Population Change

Editor: Tracy Biram

Volume 363

Independence Educational Publishers

First published by Independence Educational Publishers

The Studio, High Green

Great Shelford

Cambridge CB22 5EG

England

ISBN-13: 978 1 86168 820 0

Printed in Great Britain

Zenith Print Group

Contents

Introduction

Population Change is Volume 363 in the **ISSUES** series. The aim of the series is to offer current, diverse information about important issues in our world, from a UK perspective.

ABOUT POPULATION CHANGE

In the last two centuries the global population has risen dramatically. This book explores the changes and looks into why the population is rising and whether it will continue to do so. Also, we look at the effect population changes have on the planet and how negative the impact.

OUR SOURCES

Titles in the **ISSUES** series are designed to function as educational resource books, providing a balanced overview of a specific subject.

The information in our books is comprised of facts, articles and opinions from many different sources, including:

◆ Newspaper reports and opinion pieces

◆ Website factsheets

◆ Magazine and journal articles

◆ Statistics and surveys

◆ Government reports

◆ Literature from special interest groups.

A NOTE ON CRITICAL EVALUATION

Because the information reprinted here is from a number of different sources, readers should bear in mind the origin of the text and whether the source is likely to have a particular bias when presenting information (or when conducting their research). It is hoped that, as you read about the many aspects of the issues explored in this book, you will critically evaluate the information presented.

It is important that you decide whether you are being presented with facts or opinions. Does the writer give a biased or unbiased report? If an opinion is being expressed, do you agree with the writer? Is there potential bias to the 'facts' or statistics behind an article?

ACTIVITIES

In the back of this book, you will find a selection of activities designed to help you engage with the articles you have been reading and to explore your own opinions. Some tasks will take longer than others and there is a mixture of design, writing and research-based activities that you can complete alone or in a group.

FURTHER RESEARCH

At the end of each article we have listed its source and a website that you can visit if you would like to conduct your own research. Please remember to critically evaluate any sources that you consult and consider whether the information you are viewing is accurate and unbiased.

Useful Websites

www.eartheclipse.com

www.freedomlab.org

www.independent.co.uk

www.inews.co.uk

www.irishtimes.com

www.ons.gov.uk

www.pewresearch.org

www.populationmatters.org

www.telegraph.co.uk

www.theconversation.com

www.theguardian.com

www.worldpopulationreview.com

Overview of the UK population: August 2019

An overview of the UK population: how it has changed, why it has changed and how it is projected to change in the future.

Main points

◆ In mid-2018, the population of the UK reached an estimated 66.4 million.

◆ The UK population's growth rate in mid-2017 and mid-2018, at 0.6%, was slower than any year since mid-2004.

◆ Long-term international migration to and from the UK has remained broadly stable since the end of 2016 and has also continued to be the main driver of the UK's population growth.

◆ In 50 years' time, there is projected to be an additional 8.2 million people aged 65 years and over in the UK – a population roughly the size of present-day London.

◆ After decades of improvement to life expectancy, the latest figures show a slowdown in improvement – life expectancy at birth remained at 79.2 years for males and 82.9 years for females in 2015 to 2017.

Introduction

Understanding the size and characteristics of the UK population is vital when it comes to planning and delivering services such as education, transport and healthcare. As the UK's population continues to grow there has been a shift in the age structure towards later ages meaning we have an ageing population. In addition, our living arrangements are changing; more young adults are living with their parents and increasing numbers of people are living alone. This article brings together the main points from several bulletins to help understand how the UK's population is changing.

The UK's population continues to grow, but at a slower rate than previously

The UK population has grown year-on-year since 1982 as seen in Figure 1. The 2018 mid-year population estimates release showed that the population of the UK reached 66.4 million, up from 66.0 million in mid-2017. This population growth marks an increase of 0.6%, or an addition of 395,000 people, between mid-2017 and mid-2018 – the same rate of population growth as in the previous year. Growth in the years to mid-2017 and mid-2018 were slower than in any year since mid-2004.

Despite the recent slowdown in population growth rates, the UK population is set to increase further still. The 2016-based national population projections showed that the projected population surpasses 70.1 million by mid-2029 and reaches 72.9 million by mid-2041 – increases of 5.5% and 9.7%, respectively, from mid-2018.

All four of the UK's constituent countries (England, Northern Ireland, Scotland and Wales) continue to contribute to the UK's annual growth. England's population has continued to grow at a faster rate than the rest of the UK in the year to

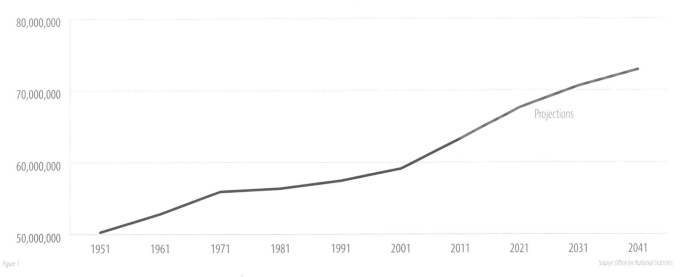

The UK's population has grown year-on-year since 1982
UK population estimates and projections, 1951 to 2041

Figure 1

Source: Office for National Statistics

mid-2018. The contributions from all the four constituent countries are as follows:

◆ England's population grew by 358,000 to 56 million (up 0.6% from mid-2017)

◆ Northern Ireland's population grew by 11,000 to 1.9 million (up 0.6% from mid-2017)

◆ Scotland's population grew by 13,000 to 5.4 million (up 0.2% from mid-2017)

◆ Wales' population grew by 13,000 to 3.1 million (up 0.4% from mid-2017)

Families and households

In this section, the following definitions are used:

◆ a family is a married, civil partnered or cohabiting couple with or without children, or a lone parent with at least one child, who live at the same address; children may be dependent or non-dependent

◆ a household is one person living alone, or a group of people (not necessarily related) living at the same address who share cooking facilities and share a living room, sitting room or dining area; a household can consist of a single family, more than one family, or no families in the case of a group of unrelated people.

As the UK's population grows, so does the number of families and households. In 2018, the number of households in the UK was 27.6 million, representing an increase of 7% from 2008 (25.9 million).

In 2018, there were 19.1 million families living in the UK, which shows an increase of 8% from 2008 (17.7 million):

◆ there were 12.8 million married couple or civil partnership families (67%)

◆ there were 3.4 million cohabiting couple families (18%)

◆ there were 2.9 million lone parent families (15%).

Cohabiting couple families are the fastest-growing family type; since 2008, there have been an additional 700,000 cohabiting couple families (a growth rate of 25.8% over this period). Meanwhile, more young adults are living with their parents. In 2018, the first age at which more than 50% of young people left the parental home was 23. Two decades earlier, more than 50% of 21-year-olds had already left home. Young men aged 20-to 34-years-old living in the UK are more likely than young women to be living with their parents (31% and 20%, respectively).

In addition, we are seeing increases in the numbers of people who are living alone – between 2008 and 2018, there has been a 6% increase (from 7.5 million to 8.0 million). This increase was driven primarily by the increase in the number of older men living alone; a 55% increase for men aged 65 to 74 years and a 20% increase for men aged 75 years and over. In 2018, nearly half of those living alone (48%) were aged 65 years and over, and more than one out of every four (27%) were aged 75 years and over.

Migration to the UK has been the main driver of population growth since the 1990s

Change in population size has four components: births, deaths, immigration and emigration.

The difference between the number of births and deaths is referred to as 'natural change'. When natural change is positive, there have been more births and deaths in the considered time frame. When it is negative, there have been more deaths than births.

The difference between the number of immigrants (people moving into the UK for more than 12 months) and the number of emigrants (people moving out of the UK for more than 12 months) is termed 'net migration'.

Natural change

In 2018, the UK experienced a natural change of 115,000 with 731,000 live births and 616,000 deaths – the lowest level of natural change since 2003.

Analysis of the births data in England and Wales in 2018 shows that the number of live births was the lowest recorded since 2005 and the birth rate was the lowest ever recorded (11.1 live births per 1,000 total population). Analysis of deaths registered in England and Wales: 2018 shows the highest

Natural change in 2018 was at its lowest level since 2013
UK births, deaths and natural change, 1951 to 2018

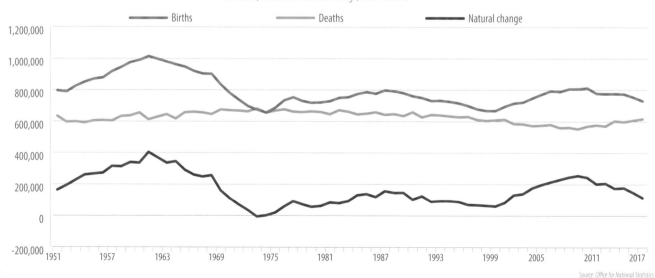

Figure 3

Source: Office for National Statistics

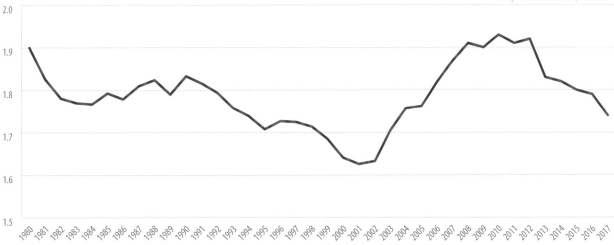

The UK Total Fertility Rate has been declining since 2012

Average number of children per woman

Figure 4   Source: Total fertility rate (TFR) calculated by the Office for National Statistics (ONS) using birth registration data and population estimates from ONS, National Records of Scotland (NRS) and Northern Ireland Statistics Research Agency (NISRA)

number of deaths since 1999 – however, when taking into account the age and size of the population, death rates have remained more or less stable since 2011.

The natural change data presented in Figure 3 are for calendar years and so will differ from the natural change component of change for the population estimates, which are calculated for mid-years (reference date 30 June).

Fluctuations in natural change have historically mirrored fluctuations in births. For example, Figure 3's left-most peak in natural change corresponds to the 1960s baby boom, which subsided in the 1970s. The second upturn in natural change is an 'echo effect' of the first, whereby baby boomers are having children of their own. Births peaked again more recently in 2012, at 813,000. Since 2012, there has been a reduction in the number of live births of 10% to 731,000, this reduction is mirrored in the reduction in natural change.

The long-term trend in the number of deaths is more stable than in the number of births. The total number of deaths peaked in 1976 at 681,000. Much of the gradual decline in the number of deaths from 1985 and 2011 has been driven by people living longer. Then as a larger number of people reach older ages there has consequently been a general increase in the number of deaths since 2011, thus contributing to the decline in natural change.

The breakdown of natural change for England, Wales and Scotland for the calendar year ending December 2018 is as follows:

◆ England's natural change was 120,000 (with 626,000 births and 506,000 deaths)

◆ Wales' natural change was negative 4,000 (with 31,000 births and 36,000 deaths)2

◆ Scotland's natural change was negative 7,000 (with 51,000 births and 59,000 deaths).

Data for Northern Ireland are available for the calendar year ending December 2017:

◆ Northern Ireland's natural change was 7,000 (with 23,000 births and 16,000 deaths)

The average number of children a woman has during her lifetime is declining

Total fertility rate (TFR) is the hypothetical average number of children a woman would have in her childbearing years if she were to experience the age-specific fertility rates of the year in question. TFR of about 2.1 children per woman is the number of children a woman would need to have to sustain current population levels (ignoring migration) – also known as the replacement fertility level.

Figure 4 displays how TFR has changed over time. The TFR hit an all-time low in 2001 for the UK with an average of 1.63 children per woman. Following this low, the TFR increased and stabilised at an average of 1.92 children per woman in 2012. In 2013, there was a substantial drop in UK TFR to 1.83. The TFR has since continued to decline – and in 2017, the average number of children per woman was 1.74.

Age-specific fertility rates show a decline in fertility rates at younger ages and rises at older ages. Between 2016 and 2017, all age groups, except women aged over 40 years, have seen decreases in fertility rates. Women aged over 40 years have continued to have higher age-specific fertility rates than those aged under 20 years.

Net migration

For the majority of the 20th century, natural change was the main driver of UK population growth, with net migration a secondary factor. In the 1990s, however, net migration increased in influence and has been the main source of growth since 1998.

Preliminary adjustments have been made to international migration estimates based on the findings from research into the coherence between migration data sources. The findings in this section are based on the preliminary adjusted estimates for the years in which they are available. Otherwise, the Long-Term International Migration (LTIM) estimates remain our best available estimates. We will continue to develop our adjustment approach in our future reports.

Long-term international migration data show that migrants continue to add to the UK population, as an estimated

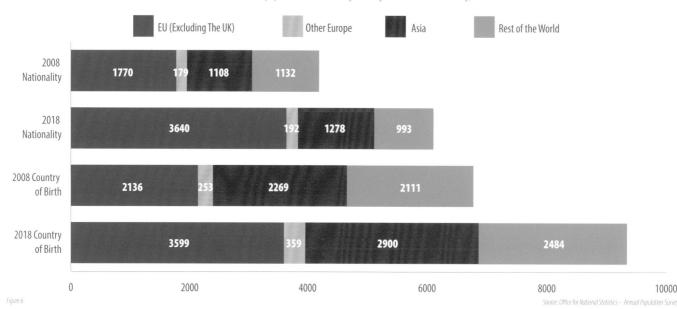

The population of non-British nationals and those born outside the UK have both increased

Non-British and non-UK-born populations of the UK by country of birth and nationality, 2008 and 2018

| | EU (Excluding The UK) | Other Europe | Asia | Rest of the World |

2008 Nationality	1770	179	1108	1132
2018 Nationality	3640	192	1278	993
2008 Country of Birth	2136	253	2269	2111
2018 Country of Birth	3599	359	2900	2484

Figure 6

Source: Office for National Statistics – Annual Population Survey

226,000 more people moved to the UK with an intention to stay 12 months or more than left in the year ending March 2019 (net migration). This is lower than the recent peak of 343,000 in the year ending June 2015; however, levels have remained broadly stable since the end of 2016. Over the last year, 612,000 people moved to the UK (immigration) and 385,000 left the UK (emigration) .

Although overall migration levels have remained broadly stable since 2016, there are different patterns for EU and non-EU citizens. EU net migration has decreased since 2015, following a three-year period of increase. Non-EU net migration has remained broadly stable over the last year, following a gradual increase since 2013.

Decisions to migrate are complex and a person's decision to move to or from the UK will always be influenced by a range of social and economic factors.

Naturally, international migration also affects the nationality and country of birth compositions of the UK. Since 2004, the resident number of non-British nationals and non-UK-born individuals has grown year-on-year (Figure 6). It is important to note that country of birth refers to the country a person was born in, so this will not change, whereas nationality is self-reported by the respondent when they are interviewed so this is subject to change.

'Country of birth' refers to the country a person was born in and can never change. 'Nationality', however, is self-reported and so can change (depending on what the individual states at their time of interview).

In 2018, about 85.7% of the UK population were UK-born and about 90.7% were British nationals – down from about 88.9% and 93.1%, respectively, in 2008.

Poland remains the most common non-UK country of birth, having taken over from India in 2015, and Polish has been the most common non-British nationality in the UK since 2008. Despite this, the largest annual decrease was seen in the Polish-born population (decreasing by 90,000 to 832,000

in 2018). Poland has also seen the largest annual decrease in nationals (decreasing by 116,000 to 905,000 in 2018).

The largest annual increases in 2018 were in the Italian-born population (increasing by 21,000 to 253,000) and Brazilian nationals (increasing by 19,000 to 59,000).

The UK's population is ageing

Like many other countries, the UK's age structure is shifting towards later ages. By 2050, it is projected that one in four people in the UK will be aged 65 years and over – an increase from approximately one in five in 2018. This is the result of the combination of declining fertility rates and people living longer. While for some living longer may be a cause for celebration, the ageing population has implications on several policy areas.

The population aged 65 years and over is growing faster than other age groups

The UK's age structure is determined by trends in fertility and mortality. Generally, both fertility and mortality rates have been declining in the UK. Thus, with less to counterbalance the living longer dynamic, the overall age structure of the UK has tipped further towards the later-life age groups.

According to projections, the population share of later-life age groups is set to increase further in future years too. By 2041, the 1960s, baby boomers will have progressed into their 70s and 80s, and by 2068 there could be an additional 8.2 million people aged 65 years and over in the UK – a population roughly the size of present-day London. This would take the UK's 65 years and over age group to 20.4 million people, accounting for 26.4% of the projected population.

In 1998, around one in six people were 65 years and over (15.9%), this increased to one in every five people in 2018 (18.3%) and is projected to reach around one in every four people (24.2%) by 2038.

Comparatively, an estimated 20.5% of the population were under 16 years old in 1998, decreasing to 19.0% in 2018 and is projected to decline to 17.4% by 2038. In 1998, 63.6% of the population were aged 16- to 64-years old, down to 62.7% in 2018 and projected to decline to 58.4% in 2038.

Within the UK, the older population make up higher proportions of the populations of rural and coastal than urban areas.

One traditional measure used to consider the impact of an ageing population is the old-age dependency ratio (OADR) – this measures the number of people of pensionable age and over per 1,000 people aged 16 years to State Pension age (SPA). In 1998, the OADR was 300; by 2008 this had increased to 307, suggesting increased dependency. In 2018, the OADR decreased to 295. However, the UK'S OADR is projected to increase into the future, reaching 360 by 2038.

While there are increases to the number of people above State Pension ages, we are seeing the number of people aged 65 years and over in work higher than ever before. Our June 2019 analysis looks at an alternative measure that takes into account the contribution of older workers. Using this alternative measure, the analysis found that economic dependency has shown an improvement, despite the population becoming older. While the main explanation is changes in economic activity, immigration of those of working age has also had some effect.

Improvements in life expectancy are slowing down

After decades of steady improvement in the UK's life expectancy, the latest figures from the National life tables show a slowdown in improvement of life expectancy in the UK. Life expectancy at birth did not improve in 2015 to 2017, when compared with 2014 to 2016 life expectancy, and remained at 79.2 years for males and 82.9 years for females. Despite no recent improvement to life expectancy, the latest figures still show the highest life expectancy the UK has seen.

On average, females continue to live longer than males; however, the gap between the sexes has decreased over the last 30 years with males seeing greater increases in life expectancy.

Within the UK, life expectancy at birth declined by 0.1 years between 2014 to 2016 and 2015 to 2017 for males and females in Scotland and Wales and for males in Northern Ireland. Life expectancy at birth remained unchanged from 2014 to 2016 for females in Northern Ireland and males and females in England.

In addition to the National life tables, we continue to monitor and report on the slowdown in life expectancy and mortality improvements in a number of publications. As we continue to see a slowdown in life expectancy improvements we will continue to analyse the data further to understand more about the causes behind this.

23 August 2019

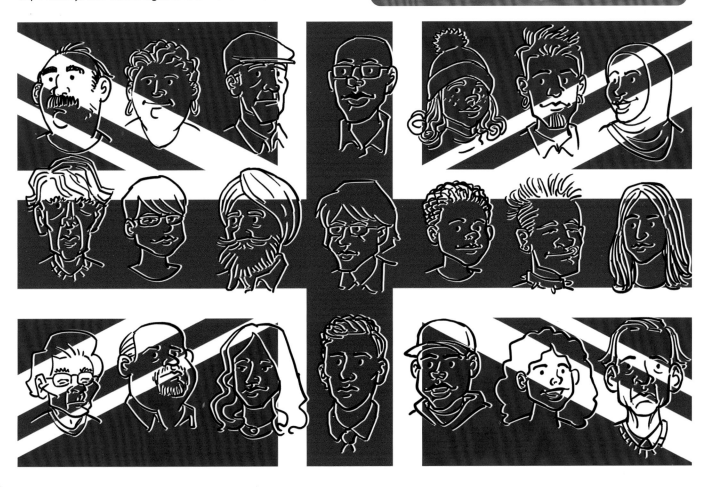

UK population set to rise by three million in next decade due to net migration increases

And major changes needed to care for ageing citizenry, charity warns.

By Conrad Duncan

The UK population is set to increase by three million within the next ten years and pass the 70 million mark in the early 2030s, according to government statistics.

The number of people in the UK is expected to rise by 4.5 per cent over the next 10 years, from an estimated 66.4 million in mid-2018 to 69.4 million in mid-2028, the Office for National Statistics (ONS) has said.

By mid-2031, the population is projected to pass 70 million, and by mid-2043, it is predicted to reach 72.4 million.

Net international migration is expected to account for 73 percent of the UK's population growth, with the ONS predicting 5.4 million people will immigrate long term to the UK between 2018 and 2028, while 3.3 million people will emigrate long-term from the UK.

During this time, 7.2 million people are predicted to be born and 6.4 million people are expected to die.

Alp Mehmet, the chairman of Migration Watch UK, said the projection was 'staggering' and warned of pressure on housing, transport, schools and university places from rising numbers.

However, the UK's population growth rate is slower than in projections made in 2016, with the expected population set to be 400,000 less in mid-2028 and 900,000 less in mid-2043 than previously predicted.

The annual population growth rate is predicted to drop from 0.6 per cent in mid-2019 to 0.27 per cent by mid-2043.

This slowdown is based on the expectation that women will have fewer children, based off recent falls in fertility rates, and a slower rate of life expectancy increases.

The UK is also expected to see a growing number of older people, with the proportion of people aged 85 or over predicted to almost double over the next 25 years.

Anna Dixon, the chief executive at the Centre for Ageing Better, said the projection showed the age of the population was 'dramatically shifting'.

'These longer lives are a huge opportunity, but big changes are needed to our workplaces, homes, health services and communities if we are to ensure that everyone is able to age well,' Ms Dixon added.

'We also need to rethink our attitudes to age, and tackle the ageist attitudes which hold back too many people from enjoying a good later life.'

England's population is anticipated to grow faster than the other UK nations, increasing by five percent between 2018 and 2028.

The ONS attributed the growth in the older population to 'baby boomers' born after the Second World War reaching older age.

'The population is increasingly ageing and this trend will continue,' the ONS said.

'However, because of the expected rise in the state pension age to 67 years, it is projected that slightly fewer than one in five people will be of pensionable age in 2028, a similar proportion to today.'

21 October 2019

Birthrate in England and Wales at all-time low

Rate drops by 46% from its ultimate peak in 1947 as 657,076 babies are born.

By Amy Walker

The birthrate in England and Wales has hit its lowest level since records began, government statistics have shown.

In total, there were 657,076 live births in England and Wales last year – a fall of 3.2% from the previous year and down by 10% from 2012.

The number of live births fell from 11.6 per 1,000 people to 11.1, the lowest since records started in 1938.

The figures, from the Office for National Statistics (ONS), also showed that the percentage of live babies with mothers not born in the UK also fell for the first time since 1990, from 28.4% to 28.2%.

Since 1947, the rate has dropped by 45.9%, when the number of babies being born was at its ultimate peak.

Although Britain's ageing population means the proportion of older people compared with women of childbearing age is increasing, the record low in crude birthrates is mostly being driven by falling fertility rates.

Except for 1977 and the period between 1999 and 2002, total fertility rates are also lower than all previous years since records began.

ONS figures show that overall fertility rates stood at 1.7 children per woman in 2018, a 3.4% decrease from the year before, when the rate was 1.76.

While crude birthrates are calculated per 1,000 of the entire population, regardless of sex or age, total fertility rates refer only to women between 15 and 44 years old, who are deemed to be of childbearing age.

Although women aged 40 and over were the only demographic for whom the rate of fertility did not fall, in 2018 the rate stalled for the first time since the 1970s, at 16.1 per 1,000.

As has been the trend since the millennium, fertility rates fell for women under 20 years of age. In 2018, the number of births per 1,000 women in the group dropped to 11.9 – down 6.3% from the previous year.

Although before 2004 women aged 25 to 29 generally had the highest fertility rate, for the past 15 years women aged 30 to 34 have taken the lead.

In 2018, stillbirths reached a record low for the second year running, with 4.1 per 1,000 total births.

Ann Berrington, a professor in demography and social statistics at the University of Southampton, said the reasons for the birthrate decline were likely to differ between age groups. As well as 'changing aspirations' she said education and expectations were among the possible reasons for fewer teenagers having babies.

'There's been government legislation which means the school leaving age has increased to 18. There's also been significant improvements in the availability of emergency and long-acting contraception,' she said.

Berrington added that she thought people in their 20s and 30s were more likely to postpone having children because of practical factors such as the lack of affordable housing.

1 August 2019

Whatever happened to 2 point 4 children?

By Nick Stripe

The phrase '2.4 children' refers to the stereotypical family size in this country. But does it still hold true? As the ONS publishes its first analysis of births that took place in England and Wales in 2018, Nick Stripe considers whether it's time to change that number.

Cast your mind back to the nineties. The era of Britpop and football coming home, where things could only get better. The sitcom *2Point4 Children*, starring Belinda Lang and Gary Olsen, introduced Bill and Ben Porter to BBC viewers on the 3 September 1991. It ran until the 30 December 1999, just as the new millennium party was getting into full swing.

Strictly speaking, Bill and Ben only had two children, David and Jenny. But dad, Ben, had juvenile tendencies which, helpfully, meant that there were 2.4 kids really. How typical were they then and now?

The broad picture painted by our analysis of births in 2018 is one of decreases and record lows. A birth rate of 11.1 births per 1,000 total population was the lowest ever recorded. And a fertility rate of 1.7 children per woman, was lower than all years except 1977 and 1999–2002.

How things have changed

At the height of the 'baby boom' in the late 1940s and mid 1960s, England and Wales was the scene of nearly 900,000 births per year. This represented a birth rate of around 20 births for every 1,000 people in the country. If the fertility rates of those years had persisted, women would, on average, have each given birth to around 2.8 children. This is known as the 'total' fertility rate. It projects forward how many children the average woman would have if she experienced that year's 'age-specific' fertility rates throughout her life.

In the years that followed, birth and fertility rates declined dramatically. By 1977, the number of births had dropped by about 300,000 compared to the mid-60s. The birth rate had fallen to 11.5 births per 1,000 people in the country. And the total fertility rate experienced in that year would have seen our average woman giving birth to 1.66 children, if it had persisted. For that one, yet to be repeated year, there were more deaths than births across England and Wales.

From the late 1970s until 1990, fertility rates gradually climbed back over 1.8 children per woman, before falling back down as we entered the new millennium. By 2001, there were fewer than 600,000 births again and the total fertility rate hit an all-time low of 1.63 children per woman.

A fairly strong recovery in births over the next ten years plateaued in the early 2010s. By then, fertility rates had risen back up to just under two children per woman.

This recovery was partly the result of an increase in fertility rates among mums born in the UK, but it also coincided with an increase in immigration. People that came to the country tended to be younger, working-age adults. And fertility rates for non-UK-born mums tend to be higher in aggregate, although this can depend on country of origin. European fertility rates are generally lower than those in England and Wales, whereas rates in countries such as Pakistan and India are higher.

Now we're at or near record lows

Which brings us back to 2018. Births, birth rates and fertility rates have been falling since 2012, a rate of decline which has accelerated in the last couple of years. We are now at or near record low levels. And we're on a downward trend.

As the total fertility rate is effectively a projection which changes from year to year, we can also look at how many children different cohorts of women have. In other words, we can take more of a backwards look too.

Trends in fertility have changed over time, not only in terms of periods of higher and lower rates, but also in terms of when women tend to have children. For example, the most common age of motherhood declined from about 25 in the post-war period, to around 22 in the early 1970s, and now stands at about 31 years of age. Given these changes to age-specific fertility rates, which form the basis of the total fertility rate, it might make more sense to look at final family sizes.

Women born between 1930 and 1940, who reached 45 years of age (the expected end of their childbearing years) between 1975 and 1985, did indeed have, on average, approximately 2.4 children. This declined to 2.2 children for women who reached 45 in the early 1990s, when Bill and Ben Porter first appeared on our screens. By the time they left them, it had declined further, to approximately two children. Women turning 45 now tend to have around 1.9 children.

So, should 1.9 be the new number?

These rates and averages include all women, including those who do not have any children. If we're thinking about families with kids, and how many kids those families have, then perhaps we should exclude women who do not have children from our calculations. This will, of course, raise the average number of children. The extent to which it's raised will depend on the number of women who remain child-free, which itself has also changed over time.

Approximately 12% of women born between 1930 and 1940 remained child-free, a figure which has ranged between 10% and 20% in the years since. Of those born in 1972, who might reasonably be expected to have finished having children now, 18% are child-free. On that basis, the average number of children born to women who have had at least one child, stands at about 2.3 for women born in the early 1970s. In which case, 2.4 could still be argued to be a valid enough number.

When it was first coined, '2.4 children' was based on the traditional nuclear family. But there are increasing numbers of people in different family units now. As well as child-free families, we have single parent families, step families, extended families, and grandparent families. So maybe it's time to put the phrase to bed?

Of course, we can't know what will happen in the future. Whether people have children and how many children they have is the result of personal, biological, social, economic, cultural, political and environmental factors. The only thing we do know about the future is that it will be different.

2 August 2019

Falling total fertility rate should be welcomed, population expert says

Figures showing declining birth rates are 'cause for celebration', not alarm.

By Nicola Davies

Declining fertility rates around the world should be cause for celebration, not alarm, a leading expert has said, warning that the focus on boosting populations was outdated and potentially bad for women.

Recent figures revealed that, globally, women now have on average 2.4 children in their lifetime, a measure known as total fertility rate (TFR). But while in some countries that figure is far higher – in Niger it is more than seven – in almost half of countries, including the UK, Russia and Japan, it has fallen to below two.

Such declines have been met with alarm, with some warning that the 'baby bust' puts countries at risk of a depopulation disaster.

But Sarah Harper, former director of the Royal Institution and an expert on population change, working at the University of Oxford, said that far from igniting alarm and panic, falling total fertility rates were to be embraced, and countries should not worry if their population is not growing.

Harper pointed out that artificial intelligence, migration, and a healthier old age, meant countries no longer needed booming populations to hold their own. 'This idea that you need lots and lots of people to defend your country and to grow your country economically, that is really old thinking,' she said.

Having fewer children is also undoubtedly positive from an environmental point of view; recent research has found that having one fewer child reduces a parent's carbon footprint by 58 tonnes of CO_2 a year.

Capping our consumption, said Harper, was crucial, not least because countries in Africa and Asia, where the fastest population rises were occurring, would need a bigger share of resources if global inequality were to be curbed.

'What we should be saying is no, [a declining total fertility rate] is actually really good because we were terrified 25 years ago that maximum world population was going to be 24 billion,' said Harper, who has three children herself. She said estimates now predicted the population would reach somewhere between 10 billion and 12 billion by the end of the century.

Declines in total fertility rate have been seen time and again after national economies develop, public health improves, and infant mortality falls, and women find themselves raising larger families. 'This is a natural process,' said Harper, adding that drivers for such declines included huge strides in family planning and women's education – with girls staying at school and entering the workforce – allowing women to delay childbearing and choose how many children to have – if any.

But there is still a ripple of alarm spreading among countries where total fertility rates have dropped below so-called replacement levels – the magic figure of 2.1.

Desperate to tackle a dearth of babies amid fears of shortages of workers and carers for the elderly, some countries have embraced incentives hoping to encourage procreation, using various methods, from matchmaking trips in Taiwan to advertising campaigns.

South Korea spent about £106 billion between 2006 and 2018 trying to encourage its population to reproduce, and although Italy's posters in 2016 proclaiming that 'Beauty knows no age… Fertility does' were taken down amid cries of sexism and even echoes of fascism, its 'fertility day'

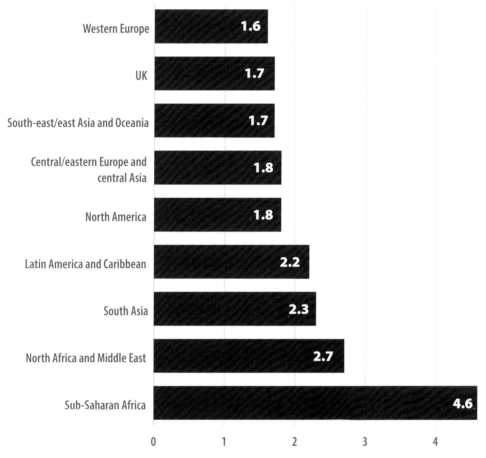

Western Europe has the lowest total fertility rate at 1.6 children per woman on average

Western Europe	1.6
UK	1.7
South-east/east Asia and Oceania	1.7
Central/eastern Europe and central Asia	1.8
North America	1.8
Latin America and Caribbean	2.2
South Asia	2.3
North Africa and Middle East	2.7
Sub-Saharan Africa	4.6

Source: Institute for Health Metrics and Evaluation 2017

remained on the calendar, with the populist government recently suggesting families could be rewarded with land for having children.

Even in China – famous for its former one-child policy – there are rumbles of concern, with academics recently proposing couples could be taxed for having too few offspring, while new hurdles are being erected to abortion and divorce.

But Harper said fears that declines in total fertility rate would see countries fall behind were groundless.

'A smaller number of highly educated people in the knowledge economy of Europe will vastly outweigh increasing our population because automation is going to take over many of the tasks,' said Harper, pointing out that AI and robotics meant work was moving away from industrial jobs, and that effort needed to be directed towards education of the young, not boosting procreation.

Changes in the military arena, she said, also undercut fears in some countries that declines in total fertility rate could leave them vulnerable – concerns that appeared to be reflected in the recent rise in the maximum age for new military recruits in Japan. 'We don't need large numbers of people for armies. Modern warfare isn't like that.'

As for dealing with an ageing society, more babies would not help much there, since children also needed to be cared for and would not enter the workforce for years.

'All the evidence is, that if families, households, societies, countries have to deal with large numbers of dependants, it takes away resources that could be put into driving society, the economy, etc.' Harper said, adding that the 'problem' of an ageing population also needed to be reconsidered, not least because technology to support dependants was advancing while people were staying in good health for longer. 'It is much easier to enable older adults to stay upskilled and healthy and in the labour market than it is to say to women "oh you have got to have children".'

Indeed, empowering women might do more to change a country's total fertility rate than pushing pro-natalism, said Harper, although that would not necessarily cause a baby boom. 'In those societies that enable women to stay in the labour market and have children, they will go from none or one child probably up to two [per woman].' In rich societies the wealthy might opt for more.

And there was another solution: movement of people – something Harper said had helped Europe and north America cope with ageing populations, boosting economies since the second world war. In Germany, women now had just 1.4 babies on average over their lifetime. 'I believe that one of the reasons why Angela Merkel took the million refugees was because she desperately needed to boost her working population,' said Harper.

It is a point that might enrage right-wing populists, but it is a powerful one. 'Migration is that wonderful balancing act,' she added.

26 December 2018

Parts of the UK are ageing twice as fast as other areas of the country as UK is 'growing apart', study warns

Parts of the UK are ageing twice as fast as other areas of the country, showing how the UK, demographically, is 'growing apart', a new study suggests.

Research by the Resolution Foundation shows that the populations of Maldon in Essex, Copeland in Cumbria and Richmondshire in Yorkshire are ageing twice as fast as the rest of the UK, while areas such as Nottingham and Oxford are growing younger.

The think tank said that while the UK population as a whole is ageing – one in four are set to be over 65 by 2041 – there is widespread demographic divergence in both the pace and direction of ageing in different areas.

The UK's average age has been rising steadily, from 36 in 1975 to 40 today. However, the report found a 25-year gap between its oldest local authority at 54-years-old and youngest, which averaged out at 29-years-old.

Charlie McCurdy, of the Resolution Foundation, said: 'Britain is growing apart as it ages because many rural and coastal communities are welcoming fewer babies each year, while migration within the UK and from abroad has seen younger people concentrating in urban areas that are already relatively young.

'This demographic divergence needs to be better understood by both policymakers and politicians, with implications for our local economies and national politics.'

The research suggested that 60 local areas across the UK have a higher typical age than Japan, the country with the highest average age of 46, including places like North Norfolk and Rother where the average age is over 50.

In contrast, Nottingham and Oxford are among 23 places in the UK that have a younger average age than Chile, which has an average age of 34, it was found.

The researchers said young people are leaving rural and coastal communities, which are already older on average than other locations, for urban areas.

Low local birth rates are also thought to be a key factor in ageing in older communities whereas poorer urban ethnically diverse areas are ageing more slowly because of high birth rates.

28 October 2019

Population change and trends in life expectancy

The population of England has increased steadily over recent decades. At the same time the population has also been ageing and in 2017, the percentage of the population aged 85 years and over was 2.7 times greater than it was in 1971.

The number of people aged 85 years and over is expected to increase substantially in the future. In 2017, there were 1.35 million people aged 85 and over in England. By 2023 this is projected to reach 1.54 million (an increase of 14%) and in 2031 (when 'baby boomers' born after World War 2 move into this age group) it could reach 2.01 million.

The ageing population is reflected in the changing distribution of deaths by age. In England and Wales in 1971, deaths among those aged 85 and over made up 15% of all deaths. By 2016 they made up 39% of all deaths.

With England's population both increasing and ageing, it was inevitable that the downward trend in number of deaths, seen since the late 1980s, could not continue indefinitely. Since 2011, when there were just over 450,000 deaths in England, the numbers have been generally increasing. By 2017 there were almost 500,000 deaths.

The number of deaths will increase considerably in the next few years if the population continues to experience recent rates of mortality. If this is the case, it is anticipated that in the year 2023 there will be around 550,000 deaths. That is just over 50,000 more deaths than in 2017, a 10% increase.

Provisional data for 2017 indicate that life expectancy at birth in England has now increased to 79.6 years for males and 83.2 years for females. People are living longer than at the start of the century, but since 2011 the rate of increase in life expectancy has slowed for both sexes. Based on life expectancy trends from 1981 to 2017, forecasts indicate that the future trend to 2023 is uncertain.

The latest data on healthy life expectancy at birth (the number of years lived in good health) show that it is now 63.3 years for males and 63.9 years for females (2014 to 2016) in England.

Since the period 2009 to 2011, life expectancy at birth has increased more than healthy life expectancy and therefore the number of years lived in poor health has increased slightly, as has the proportion of life spent in poor health. In the period 2014 to 2016, males lived 16.2 years in poor health, while females lived 19.3 years in poor health.

In 2016, UK life expectancy at birth was above the European Union (EU) average for males, but below the EU average for females. For both sexes, since 2011 it has improved more slowly in the UK than the EU average. However, with the exception of Italy, all of the six largest EU member states have seen a reduction in the rate of improvement in life expectancy since 2011.

Introduction

Average life expectancy has increased in England in recent decades, as presented in the Health Profile for England 2017.

Less than a century ago, deaths from infectious diseases were common and often death would follow a relatively short period of illness. However, chronic non-communicable diseases are now the leading causes of death and long

Trend in percentage of deaths by age, England and Wales, 1971, 1980, 2000 and 2016

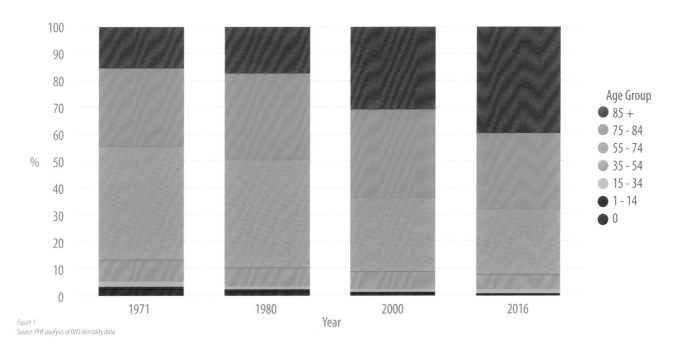

Figure 1
Source: PHE analysis of ONS mortality data

periods of moderate and severe ill health often precede death.

We have an ageing population: in England in 2017, 1.35 million people were aged 85 and over, almost half a million of whom were in their 90s. The size of the population at older ages is important as the older a person is, the more likely they are to live with chronic conditions such as dementia, diabetes and some musculoskeletal conditions.

The size of the population aged 85 years and over is, therefore, an important determinant of demand for health and social care as older people have the highest usage.

As well as looking at population changes, this article updates analysis in the Health Profile for England 2017 and looks at trends in the following measures:

◆ life expectancy (the average number of years that an individual is expected to live based on current mortality rates)

◆ healthy life expectancy (the average number of years that an individual is expected to live in a state of good or very good health, based on current mortality rates and prevalence of self-assessed good or very good health)

◆ average number of years lived in poor health (the difference between life expectancy and healthy life expectancy)

◆ proportion of life spent in poor health (number of years in poor health as a percentage of life expectancy).

Average life expectancy and healthy life expectancy are both important headline measures of the health status of the population. The healthy life expectancy measure adds a 'quality of life' dimension to estimates of life expectancy by dividing them into time spent in different states of health. The number of years of life in poor health is also important as it relates more closely to demand for health and social care, and associated costs.

When comparing outcomes for groups with very different life expectancies, the proportion of life spent in poor health is also useful. Two populations may both spend on average 15 years in poor health, which might be a quarter of life for a group with life expectancy of 60, but only a sixth of life for a group with life expectancy of 90.

Population change and trends in the number of deaths

The total population of England has increased steadily over recent decades. At the same time the population has also been ageing and the number of people aged 85 years and over has increased. In 2017 the proportion of the population aged 85 years and over was 2.7 times greater than it was in 1971.

The distribution of deaths by age group has changed as the population has aged. In 1971, deaths among those aged 85 years and over made up just 15% of all deaths in England and Wales, but by 2016 they accounted for 39% of the total (Figure 1). In 1971, the number of deaths at ages 85 years and over was six times as great as the number of deaths under age one. In 2016, there were 76 times more deaths at age 85 years and over than under age one.

Despite an increasing and ageing population, a general decline in the annual number of deaths in England started in the late 1980s. In 1995, there were almost 530,000 deaths in England but by 2011 this had reduced to just over 450,000

With England's population both growing and ageing, it was however inevitable that the downward trend in the number of deaths could not continue indefinitely. Since 2011 the numbers have been generally increasing and by 2017 there were almost 500,000 deaths in England.

To provide an indication of the future size and age structure of the population, the Office for National Statistics (ONS) produces regular sets of population projections. These are

Trend in life expectancy at birth, males and females, England, 1981 to 2017, projections and forecasts from 2018 to 2023

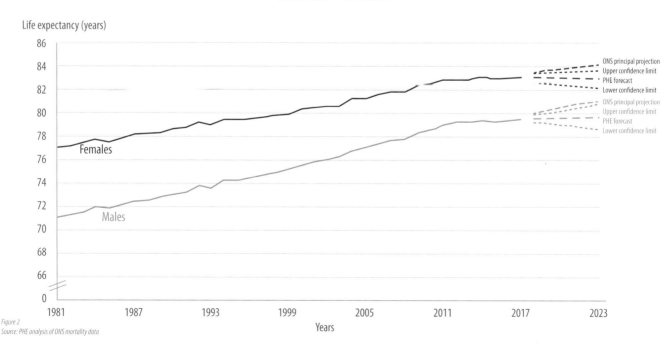

Figure 2
Source: PHE analysis of ONS mortality data

based on assumptions of what will happen in the future with levels of births, deaths and migration.

The number of people aged 85 years and over is projected to increase substantially in the future. In 2017, there were 1.35 million people aged 85 and over in England. By 2023, this is projected to increase by 14% to 1.54 million. Between 2023 and 2031 (when those 'baby boomers' born immediately after World War 2 will reach 85), the population aged 85 and over is projected to increase by 31% to 2.01 million.

From their current principal projections, ONS estimate that there would be around 502,000 deaths in England by 2023. This is based on an assumption that mortality rates will fall in the future. ONS also produce an alternative set of projections which assume that mortality rates in the future will not improve but will stay at the same level as in 2016. From these, ONS estimate that there will be around 550,000 deaths in 2023, just over 50,000 more than the number in 2017.

Later sections of this article will show how there has been relatively little improvement in mortality rates in England since 2011. If mortality rates were to rise in the future, the number of deaths could be even higher than those in the ONS projections.

Trends in life expectancy at birth

Life expectancy at birth in England has increased in recent decades and provisional data for 2017 show that it has reached 79.6 years for males and 83.2 years for females (Figure 2). This is an increase of 0.1 years, since 2016, for both males and females. Male life expectancy has increased

faster than that for females and the gap in life expectancy is now less than four years, whereas in 1981 it was six years.

Life expectancy at birth for males increased by an average of 13.9 weeks per year from 1981 to 2011, while for females the increase was 10.3 weeks per year (Figure 2). Between 2011 and 2017, the average increase in life expectancy slowed for both sexes, to 4.3 weeks per year for males and 1.7 weeks for females. There has thus been a reduction in the rate of improvement in life expectancy since 2011.

ONS produces regular projections of life expectancy which are derived by estimating long-term trends in mortality improvement and projecting them forward for future decades. The latest principal projections from ONS (which assume that mortality rates will fall in the future) project that in 2023 life expectancy at birth will be 81.1 years for males and 84.3 years for females (Figure 2), an increase of 9.4 weeks and 7.3 weeks per year respectively, over the period of the projection (2018 to 2023).

Besides the principal projections of life expectancy illustrated in Figure 2, ONS also produce high and low life expectancy variants, which respectively assume more and less improvement in mortality rates. If it is assumed that mortality rates remain constant then life expectancy would also remain constant.

PHE have produced life expectancy forecasts based on fitting a model to the trends in life expectancy from 1981 to 2017. These forecasts show that the more slowly rising trend since 2011 has not been observed for long enough to be clear whether it will continue. The upper and lower

Breakdown of change in life expectancy at birth by age, males and females, England, 2001 to 2006, 2006 to 2011 and 2011 to 2016

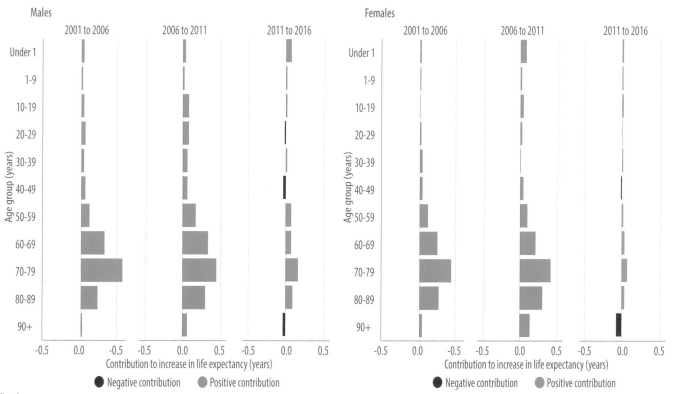

Figure 3
Source: PHE analysis of ONS data

Trend in life expectancy at birth, males and females, countries of the UK, 2006 to 2016

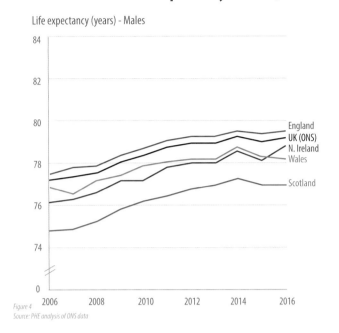

Life expectancy (years) - Males

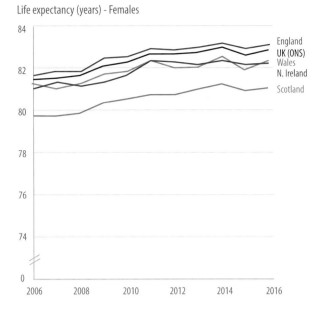

Life expectancy (years) - Females

Figure 4
Source: PHE analysis of ONS data

confidence limits shown around the forecasts indicate that the future trend is uncertain for both sexes.

Breakdown of trends in life expectancy at birth by age

The contribution of different age groups to the change in life expectancy between time points can be assessed using a method of 'decomposition'.

Contributions that increased life expectancy (that is, where the mortality rate has reduced over time) have a positive value, while contributions that offset the life expectancy increase (where the mortality rate has increased over time) have a negative value (Figure 3).

All age groups made a positive contribution to improvements in life expectancy between 2001 and 2006, and between 2006 and 2011. The age groups which made the biggest contribution to improvements were the older ages, 60 to 89.

The contribution from almost all age groups was smaller between 2011 and 2016, indicating that the slowdown in mortality improvement occurred across most age groups. For both sexes, some age groups made a negative contribution to the change in life expectancy, as indicated by the red bars in the charts. The most noticeable negative contribution was for females aged 90 years and over.

Healthy life expectancy at birth

Data for healthy life expectancy are published by ONS as three-year averages (for example, 2014 to 2016). Since 2009 to 2011 there has been no significant change to healthy life expectancy in England and data for 2014 to 2016 indicate that it is now 63.3 years for males and 63.9 years for females.

Although females live longer than males, in 2014 to 2016 there was little difference in healthy life expectancy between the sexes. Females, therefore, spent more years in poor health than males (19.3 years compared with 16.2 years for males) and a greater proportion of life in poor health (23.2% compared with 20.4%).

The majority of the extra years of life for females in 2014 to 2016 were spent in poor health: females lived 3.6 years longer than males but had only 0.6 years longer in good health. Therefore three of these extra years were spent in poor health.

In the Health Profile for England 2017, an increase in male healthy life expectancy of 2.8 years was reported between 2000 to 2002 and 2012 to 2014. The increase for females was 1.5 years. Due to a change in methodology, comparable data for recent years are now only available back to 2009 to 2011. This short time frame limits the conclusions that can be made about trends, as indicators giving a summary picture of population health tend to change slowly.

Male life expectancy at birth increased by 0.8 years between 2009 to 2011 and 2014 to 2016, and healthy life expectancy increased by 0.3 years. Years spent in poor health thus increased by 0.5 years. The proportion of life lived in poor health increased slightly: 20.0% in 2009 to 2011; 20.4% in 2014 to 2016.

For females between 2009 to 2011 and 2014 to 2016, life expectancy at birth increased by 0.4 years but healthy life expectancy fell by 0.2 years, so years lived in poor health increased by 0.7 years. The proportion of life lived in poor health increased from 22.5% in 2009 to 2011, to 23.2% in 2014 to 2016.

It is important to note that this measure of years spent in poor health is self-reported and does not adjust for the severity of ill health or the types of conditions that may be present.

Life expectancy and healthy life expectancy at age 65

The trend in life expectancy at age 65 years has been upwards in recent decades. In 2014 to 2016, males aged 65 lived a further 18.8 years (up from 16.3 years in 2001 to 2003) and females an additional 21.1 years (up from 19.2 years in 2001 to 2003).

Trend in life expectancy at birth, males and females, largest EU member states, 2006 to 2016

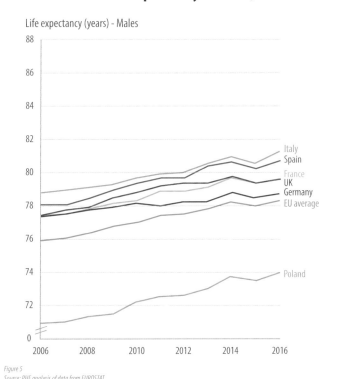

Life expectancy (years) - Males

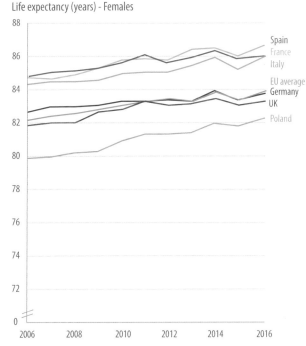

Life expectancy (years) - Females

Figure 5
Source: PHE analysis of data from EUROSTAT

Since 2009 to 2011, increases in life expectancy have slowed for both sexes at age 65 and increases in healthy life expectancy have kept pace, so the number of years lived in poor health has remained about the same. Males lived 8.2 years in poor health from age 65 in both 2009 to 2011 and 2014 to 2016, while females lived 10.0 years in poor health in 2009 to 2011 and 9.8 years in 2014 to 2016.

The proportion of life from age 65 spent in poor health was 44.0% for males and 46.6% for females in 2014 to 2016.

UK comparisons

Of the four UK nations, England had the highest life expectancy for both males and females in 2016. This has consistently been the case in recent years (Figure 4). All four nations have experienced a slowing of life-expectancy improvement since 2011, and all had a decrease in life expectancy for both sexes in 2015.

European comparisons

Female life expectancy is doing comparatively worse than male life expectancy when compared with the rest of the European Union (EU). Among the 28 EU member states in 2016, the UK was ranked 10th highest for male life expectancy but only 17th for female life expectancy. UK male life expectancy was above the EU average but was 1.6 years lower than the highest country (Italy). However, female life expectancy in the UK was lower than the EU average and 3.3 years lower than Spain, the country with the highest level in 2016.

These comparisons are made with the UK rather than England as it is the UK which is the EU member state. In addition, it is not possible to compare England with the EU as the EU data are calculated using a method which is not directly comparable to the method used by ONS to calculate life expectancy in England.

Between 2011 and 2016, the average annual increase in life expectancy in the EU as a whole was lower than the increase between 2006 and 2010, for males and females. With the exception of Italy, all of the six largest EU member states had a smaller annual improvement over the later period.

The average annual improvement in life expectancy in the UK between 2011 and 2016 was lower than in the other largest EU member states, and lower than the EU average, for both sexes. All of the largest EU member states had a fall in life expectancy in 2015 (Figure 5).

Data is also available on healthy life expectancy for all EU member states, based on responses to a survey question asking how respondents rate their health in general. In 2016, throughout the EU, although males lived shorter lives than females, they spent a smaller proportion of their lives in poor health. This suggests that the bulk of the extra years of life for females were spent in poor health.

In 2016, the proportion of life spent in poor health was smaller in the UK than the EU average, except for males at birth. At age 65, both males and females in the UK spent a smaller proportion of life in poor health than the other large EU countries.

11 September 2018

Life expectancy rises for babies born between 2016 and 2018 but overall increase is slowing, says ONS

Latest figures reveal slight increase of around a month on previous three-year period.

People in the UK are living longer than ever, after latest figures revealed life-expectancy levels have increased for both men and women.

A child born between 2016 and 2018 can expect to live to 79.3 if they are male and 82.9 if they are female, according to the Office for National Statistics (ONS).

It found life expectancy at birth had improved slightly since the last three-year period of 2015–17, rising by 3.7 weeks for men and 4.2 weeks for women.

Slow increases

However, the ONS said the relatively slow increases showed that the slowdown in life-expectancy improvements which has been noted since 2011 was continuing.

'Between 2016 and 2018 we have seen much lower increases than experienced in previous decades. Nevertheless, life expectancy is increasing,' said Edward Morgan, from the ONS Centre for Ageing and Demography.

'The causes behind the overall slowdown are likely to be complex.

'As we see another year of low life-expectancy improvements, we will continue our work to understand more about the causes behind this.'

The ONS said the probability of reaching the age of 90 remained the same, with one in five boys and one in three girls born between 2016 and 2018 expected to reach the milestone.

However, it found the number of people currently reaching 100 or more had gone down, with 13,170 centenarians alive in 2018 – a drop of 5 per cent on the previous year.

The ONS said this had been fuelled by the lower number of births during the First World War and that there was expected to be a big jump in their number in the future.

Reaching 100

It said this was because the number of births spiked in the latter half of 1919 following the return of soldiers from the conflict.

Some 45.4 per cent more babies were born across the UK between mid-1919 and mid-1920 than in the year before, it said.

The UN has estimated there were 499,198 centenarians in the world in 2018, comprised of 106,013 males and 393,185 females.

In the UK in 2018, there were seven male centenarians per 100,000 population of males and 33 female centenarians per 100,000 population of females.

25 September 2019

How many humans tomorrow? The United Nations revises its projections

An article from The Conversation.

THE CONVERSATION

By Gilles Pison, Anthropologue et démographe, professeur au Muséum national d'histoire naturelle et chercheur associé à l'INED, Muséum national d'histoire naturelle (MNHN)

In 2019 the planet has 7.7 billion inhabitants, which is likely to rise to 8.5 billion in 2030 and nearly ten billion in 2050. These figures are taken from the world population projections just released by the United Nations.

They correspond to the medium scenario in which fertility, which is 2.5 children per woman today worldwide and decreases year by year, continues to decline to 2.2 children in 2050 and 1.9 in 2100. Under the high scenario, fertility declines less rapidly, with a level of 0.5 children above the medium scenario, and the world population would reach 10.6 billion by 2050. In the low scenario, it decreases faster and is 0.5 children below the medium scenario, with the population reaching only 8.9 billion by 2050. Extending the projections leads to 10.9 billion inhabitants in 2100 in the medium scenario and, respectively, 16 and s billion in the high and low scenarios (Figure 1).

3% fewer people in 2100 than projected two years ago

These new projections replace those that the United Nations published in 2017. The calculations have been revised upwards or downwards according to the countries or regions. For example, in the medium scenario, the figure for China in 2100 is 44 million higher than that in the 2017 projections (4% more). In contrast, for India, it is down 66 million (4% less). The same goes for Africa as a whole, whose projected population in 2100 is reduced by 187 million (-4%). For the planet as a whole, the upward and downward revisions offset each other, but only partly. According to the medium scenario, the global total for 2050 is projected to be 37 million fewer people than in the previous projections (-0.4%) and 309 million fewer in 2100 (-3%).

The UN revises its population projections every two years. Like those just released, the changes from the projections released two years earlier look small. But when accumulated over several decades, they become significant.

Projections have changed a lot in 40 years

The first time the United Nations published population projections up to 2100 was in 1981, and their medium scenario predicted then that the world population would reach 10.5 billion that year. The June 2019 projections

World population since 1900 and projections up to 2100

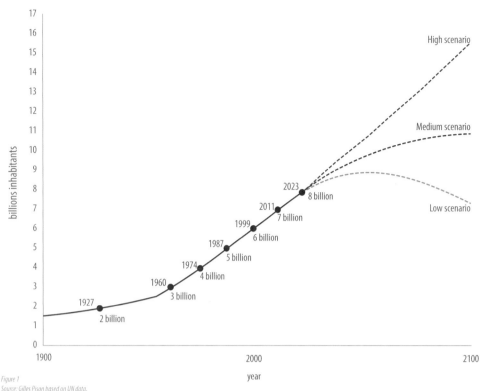

Figure 1
Source: Gilles Pison based on UN data.

Mortality has declined more than expected

Where do these changes come from? The population of a country or continent changes because of fertility and mortality. Migration is also a factor, but to a lesser extent for many countries and with zero effect worldwide. It is therefore the assumptions on mortality and fertility that affect projections. For mortality, it declined faster than imagined 40 years ago, especially for children, which led to more rapid growth. The AIDS epidemic was certainly not anticipated at the time, and Africa has paid the heaviest cost. But the excess mortality it has caused will have lasted only one-time, and life expectancy has begun to increase again in recent years and relatively quickly. AIDS has had little effect on the demographic vitality of Africa.

suggest a figure of 10.9 billion – 0.4 billion higher. While the world total is slightly higher, it conceals a radical change in population distribution across the different continents. In 1981, the population of Asia was projected to reach 5.9 billion by 2100, but in 2019 the figure was revised downward to 4.7 billion (20% less). Likewise, for Latin America, the figure of 1,187 million in 2100 was lowered to 680 million (a decrease of about 43%). For Africa, on the other hand, the 1981 projections were 2.2 billion for 2100, while the 2019 projections have nearly doubled this figure to 4.3 billion (see Figure 2 below).

The changes in assumptions that ultimately had the larger effect on the projections are those concerning fertility, the evolution of which was revised following various surprises.

Replacement of generations?

Nearly 40 years ago, the UN's medium scenario population projections were based on future fertility of close to 2.1 children per woman everywhere in the world. In countries

Projections published in 1981 (medium scenario)

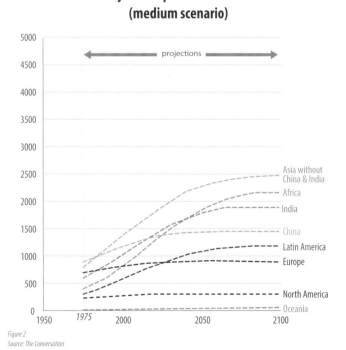

Figure 2
Source: The Conversation

Projections published in 2019 (medium scenario)

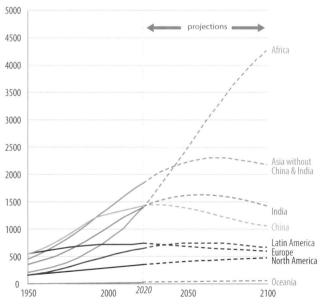

Fertility trends by world region from 1950 to 2020 and projections up to 2100
(United Nations medium scenario)

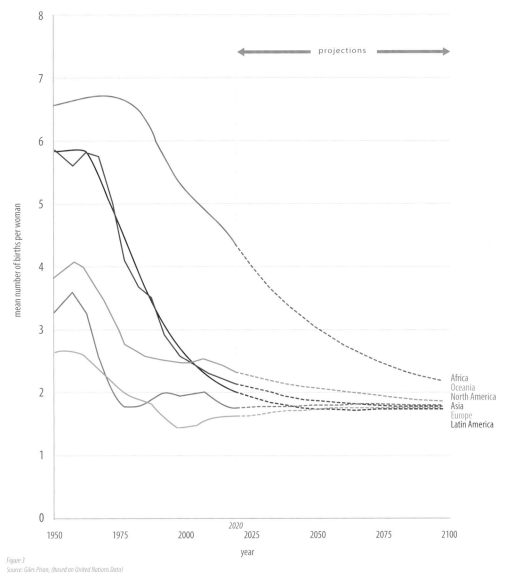

Figure 3
Source: Giles Pison, (based on United Nations Data)

have joined the countries of the North in low fertility. Consequently, the United Nations has abandoned its hypothesis of convergence to 2.1 children to adopt a convergence level well below: 1.85 children (Figure 3). The population curves then has a bell-like shape almost everywhere: after reaching a maximum, the population decreases (Figure 2).

The second surprise came 30 years ago, when surveys revealed the unexpectedly rapid pace of fertility decline in many countries of Asia and Latin America. In response to this new trend, the United Nations made substantial downward revisions to their demographic projections for these continents.

A third, more recent surprise concerns intertropical Africa. Fertility decline in this region was expected to begin later than in Asia and Latin America due to slower social and economic development, but it was assumed that the rate of decrease would be similar to that assumed for other regions of the Global South.

This is indeed the case in North and Southern Africa but not in intertropical Africa, where the fertility decline is occurring more slowly. This explains the upward revision of projections for Africa, which could be home to more than a third of the world's population by 2100.

already below this – like most industrialised countries – it was forecast to rise incrementally to 2.1, then flatten out. In higher fertility countries, it was projected to fall to 2.1 and then level off.

This threshold corresponds to the replacement of generations – each couple is replaced on average by two children becoming adults themselves – and choosing it as the level of convergence assumes a long-term stabilisation of the world's population as well as that of each region composing it. Hence, in the 1981 projections, each region's or country's population curve plateaus once the growth phase has ended (Figure 2).

The evolution of fertility

However, the observed fertility trends were different and the scenarios had to be revised to take into account several surprises.

First surprise: fertility has remained well below 2.1 children in many industrialized countries. And many Southern countries

These figures are projections, and the future is not written. However, demographic projections are quite reliable for predicting population size in the short-term future, i.e. over periods of 10, 20 or 30 years. As for more distant projections, they will undoubtedly be revised following the surprises that the future holds for us.

17 June 2019

What is overpopulation?

By Sonia Madaan

Overpopulation is the state whereby the human population rises to an extent exceeding the carrying capacity of the ecological setting. In an overpopulated environment, the numbers of people might be more than the available essential materials for survival such as transport, water, shelter, food or social amenities. This regularly contributes to environmental deterioration, worsening in the quality of life, or even the disintegration of the population.

It is estimated that about 81 million people add to the world's population annually. Regions with the highest number of population density (the number of people living in a given region) feel the dire effects and problems of overpopulation. Due to immigration, the decline in mortality rates, medical breakthroughs, and increased birth rates, populations will always increase and eventually gives rise to overpopulation.

Wikipedia defines overpopulation as;

'Overpopulation occurs when a population of a species exceeds the carrying capacity of its ecological niche. Overpopulation is a function of the number of individuals compared to the relevant resources, such as the water and essential nutrients they need to survive. It can result from an increase in births, a decline in mortality rates, an increase in immigration, or an unsustainable biome and depletion of resources.'

Problems of overpopulation

Overpopulation thus contributes to some of the most compelling environmental problems which encompass:

Depletion of natural resources

As human population keeps on enlarging, exhaustible natural resources such as arable land, coral reefs, fresh water, fossil fuels, and wilderness forests continue to drop sharply. This creates competitive demands on the vital life-sustaining resources and contributes to an incredible decline in the quality of life.

According to a study by the UNEP Global Environment Outlook, excessive human consumption of the naturally occurring non-renewable resources can outstrip available resources in the near future and remarkably deplete them for future generations.

Accelerated habitat loss

The increased loss of the ecosystems including wetlands, wildlife, rainforests, coral reefs, aquatic life forms, and grasslands are highly influenced by overpopulation. It is out of overpopulation that activities such as excessive agriculture, environmental pollution, and extensive land development have become more and more intensive.

For example, rainforests originally covered 14% of the entire earth's surface. Today, rainforest only cover about 6% of the earth's surface and scientists' project it may even become less in the next four decades judged by the current rate of vegetation removal, logging, and deforestation. Besides, due to environmental pollution, 30% of the ocean reefs have been lost because of acidification and global warming since 1980. Also, more than half of the original wetlands have been lost.

Amplified climate change and global warming

Because of overpopulation, it means more and more population. The more the number of people, the more the number of vehicles and industries as well as air travels. Furthermore, more population translates to increased use of energy sources such as coal and firewood which contributes to increased greenhouse gas emissions.

Hence, because of the accumulation of human-generated greenhouse gases and carbon footprint in the atmosphere, the planet has continued to witness amplified global warming and climate change. The effects of climate change and global warming are profound resulting in extreme hunger, drought, flooding, and habitat loss to an extent of threatening the survival of human civilisation.

Loss of biodiversity

Overpopulation has seen continued encroachment into frontier forests, heightened pollution, and destruction of natural ecosystems that has greatly contributed to the mass extinction of species. The number of threatened species persists to multiply worldwide, whereas some have completely gone extinct.

This is because of the human activities such as acidifying water systems, over-exploitation of natural resources, pollution, over-fishing, poaching, and the deliberate as well as the indirect destruction of natural systems necessary for the survival of different species. These human activities simply alter the natural process combined, thus destroying the natural ecosystems supporting biodiversity.

Depreciation of fresh water

The unrelenting nature of overpopulation on earth has destroyed most of the world's freshwater systems. Most of the lakes, streams, rivers and groundwater making up fresh water have been made unreachable or become too polluted. According to the global outlook of water resources, these activities influenced by overpopulation have only left less than 1% of the planet's freshwater readily accessible for human utilisation.

Water vulnerability is already affecting many overpopulated nations, especially in some developing countries, as the demands for water tend to be more than the accessible water. Millions of fish species from freshwater ecosystems are on the verge of extinction. Thus, as human inhabitants rise in number, so will the problem of quality freshwater accessibility.

Lower life expectancy and diminished quality of life

Overpopulation lowers the standards of living since it creates stress on the vital resources for survival and increases the difficulty of accessing the consistent supply of quality food, water, energy, health, security and shelter. Consequently, it makes the poor to become poorer, and they often opt for poor living conditions to survive.

Eventually, it gives rise to lower life expectancy. The situation is serious in developing nations such as southern Asia and sub-Saharan Africa where most of the poor populations submit to inadequate and poor diets.

Emergence of new pandemics and epidemics

According to WHO, overpopulation is one of the leading causes of the speedy occurrence and emergence of human diseases. Overpopulation worsens numerous environmental and social factors such as pollution, malnutrition, overcrowded living conditions, and lacking health care which makes poor communities vulnerable to infectious diseases. Diseases such as tuberculosis, malaria, HIV, and dysentery spread faster in overpopulated areas.

Intensive farming practices

In regions where populations are high, people resort to farming practices that can produce more food products with cheaper inputs and without encroaching into surrounding lands due to the recent environmental protection policies. Intensive farming has thus resulted, and it has led to soil fertility depletion, re-emergence of parasites, the emergence of new parasites, loss of ecosystems, pollution of water systems, and decreased biodiversity.

Rise in unemployment, crime rate, and violence

In overpopulated nations, the available jobs are fewer than the overall job-seeking population. This contributes to high levels of unemployment. In turn, lack of unemployment leads to elevated crime rates because of theft, drug cartels, and militia groups, which are exploited as options for attaining basic resources and necessities such as food, good living standards, and wealth. Violence and conflicts arise when people start competing for the available limited resources.

Global risks: where does population rank?

An online survey of over 10,000 adults across nine countries found that more than two-thirds of respondents consider population growth a 'global catastrophic risk'. However, less than a quarter believe the issue requires urgent action and just over half believe continued population growth will have 'negative effects', down from 64% in 2017. One in two people wrongly believes that there are sufficient natural resources for all humans to live like those in rich countries.

Overall, it is very positive that most people think of population growth as a threat but there is clearly still a strong need to raise awareness of the urgency of the issue.

Falling population concern

The *Attitudes to global risk and governance survey 2018*, a follow-up to the 2017 version, was commissioned by the Global Challenges Foundation (GCF) and is intended to assess public perception of major global issues such as climate change, conflict and population growth. Between April 2017 and April 2018, over 1,000 people aged 18–64 took part in Australia, Brazil, China, Germany, India, Russia, South Africa, Sweden, the United Kingdom and the United States.

Overall, six in ten respondents considered the world to be more dangerous in 2018 than two years ago. Politically motivated violence was thought to be the most concerning global risk, particularly among developed countries. This is understandable in light of the growing instability in Europe and ongoing conflicts in countries like Syria, Ukraine, and North Korea.

The proportion of people who consider population growth a global catastrophic risk has decreased from 80% in 2017 to 70% today and only 23% now believe the issue warrants urgent action, compared to a third of respondents in 2017.

Developing countries are more aware

Developing countries tended to be more worried than developed countries about climate change (86% vs 80%) and other environmental damage (89% vs 81%). Respondents in developing countries, in particular India and South Africa, were also more concerned about population growth. In India, population growth was ranked the fourth most-important global catastrophic risk. This is unsurprising as fast-growing, vulnerable countries are more exposed to the negative impacts of overpopulation, climate change, pollution and other damage.

Only a few believe growth is good

The only country where respondents deemed the world to be more secure now than two years ago was China, where population growth has reached an all-time low. This trend was driven by millennials, which were 44% more likely to say that the world is safer now than baby boomers.

UK millennials were more likely to think that the consequences of population growth will be positive (16% vs 1% of baby boomers). Worryingly, highly educated UK adults were more likely than those with a low level of education to think that the consequences of population growth will be positive for humankind (13% vs 7%). While one in ten is not very many, this does demonstrate the damage that is being done by intentional dismissal of the problem

Concern over population growth has fallen substantially

Perceptions of various issues as global catastrophic risks, NET agree (Strongly + tend to), all respondents

Issue	%
Politically motivated violence and conflict escalating into war	88%
Usage of weapons of mass destruction	85%
Other large-scale environmental damage	85%
Climate change	83%
Natural epidemics and pandemics	75%
Population growth	70%
The rise of artificial intelligence	53%

Source: Population Matters

Required urgency of response to population growth has gone down substantially

Perceived urgency of response, risks ranked in top 3 most urgent, by country, all countries

2017 Required urgency of response			2018 Required urgency of response		
%	Theme	Rank	%	Theme	Rank
62%	Usage of WMDs	1	64%	Usage of WMDs	1
57%	Politically motivated violence	2	61%	Politically motivated violence	2
56%	Climate change	3	53%	Climate change	3
40%	Other environmental damage	4	38%	Other environmental damage	4
37%	Epidemics and pandemics	5	36%	Epidemics and pandemics	5
32%	Population growth	6	23%	Population growth	6
16%	Artificial intelligence	7	15%	Artificial intelligence	7

In India environmental issues take precedent

Top 5 most important global catastrophic risks

91%
Other environmental damage

90%
Climate change

86%
Politically motivated violence

86%
Population growth

86%
Weapons of mass destruction

Source: Population Matters

of overpopulation. In a similar international GCF survey conducted in 2014, the public tended to consider population growth as a threat, whereas policy makers overwhelmingly did not. In many developed countries, politicians are calling for more, not fewer, births to counter population ageing and boost economic growth.

Misconceptions about natural resources

Concern over resource shortage has also decreased relative to 2017, with almost half of respondents believing that the world's natural resources are sufficient for all of Earth's people to enjoy the same standard of living as in rich countries. This is a huge misconception. According to the Global Footprint Network, we are currently consuming 1.7 Earth's worth of resources and would need five planets if everyone consumed as much as the average US citizen.

Governments and educational institutions are failing in their duty to raise awareness of the urgency of the environmental crisis and its link to overpopulation. Despite the severe shortage of education opportunities in developing countries, these tend to be more aware because they are more exposed to negative impacts.

It is reassuring that the strong majority of people still think of population growth as a risk, but all countries, particularly those which are affluent and sheltered from the worst effects of climate change and overpopulation, must do more to raise awareness and implement ethical and progressive measures to counter unsustainable population growth.

15 February 2019

Consumption of Earth's resources

Number of Earths needed if everyone used renewable resources at the same rate as these individual countries

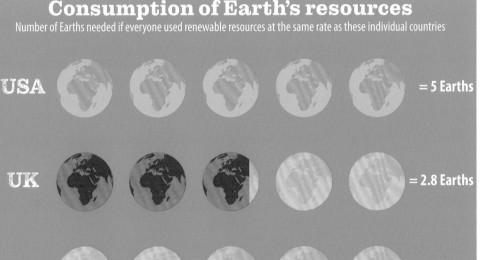

USA = 5 Earths

UK = 2.8 Earths

China = 2.1 Earths

Niger = 1 Earths

India = 0.7 Earths

Source: Global Footprint Network, 2018

www.populationmatters.org

Earth's population may start to fall from 2040. Does it matter?

William Reville: As populations age and are not replenished, societies could be strained.

The conventional projection by the UN is that world population, currently 7.7 billion, will increase to 11.2 billion in 2100, then stabilise before slowly declining. However, current trends cast much doubt on this picture. Fertility rates are in dramatic decline worldwide and world population may peak below nine billion by 2050 and then decline.

In order for a human population to maintain its numbers, each woman must bear, on average, 2.1 children. If the birth rate exceeds 2.1, population numbers increase; if it is less than 2.1, population numbers decline. Birth rates below 2.1 have been common now since 1970. Ireland had a birth rate of 1.92 in 2016 but inward migration is contributing to population growth.

The *UN World Fertility Patterns 2015* Report details birth rates (children per woman) for the major world regions – Africa 4.7, Asia 2.2, Europe 1.6, Latin America/Caribbean 2.2, North America 1.9, Oceania 2.4. The overall world fertility rate is 2.5. So world population numbers continue to grow.

> 'India, with a fertility rate of 2.1, will soon overtake China as the world's most populous nation'

World population trends were reviewed recently by Darrell Bricker and John Ibbitson in *The Observer* on 27 January. The authors seriously questioned the UN projection that world population numbers would continue to increase until 2100, quoting several well-respected demographers. Jorgen Randers, a Norwegian academic who decades ago warned of a potential global catastrophe caused by overpopulation, has changed his mind.

'The world population will never reach nine billion people,' he now believes. 'It will peak at eight billion in 2040 and then decline.' Similarly, Prof. Wolfgang Lutz and his fellow demographers at Vienna's International Institute for Applied Systems Analysis predict the human population will stabilise by mid-century and then start to go down.

European decline

The populations of many countries shrink every year. For example, Japan's dropped 450,000 in 2018. Many of the fastest-shrinking populations are in eastern Europe. The following countries are examples where populations are in decline (fertility rates in brackets, but population decline is often increased by emigration) – Bulgaria (1.58), Greece (1.3), Hungary (1.39), Italy (1.49), Poland (1.29), Portugal (1.24), Russia (1.75), Japan (1.48) and South Korea (1.26).

Declining fertility rates, combined with increasing life expectancy, generate societies enriched in older people and depleted in younger people. This strains society's ability to generate the wealth and taxes necessary to fund the welfare state and healthcare for the elderly.

There are several reasons why birth rates have plummeted in the developed world. For example, full-time careers are now the norm for women. I come from a family of five children and my mother worked full time in the home. Both my wife and I have always worked careers and we have two children. People also tend to have fewer children now because of better healthcare – every child born is expected to survive. And, of course, contraception is universally available nowadays.

Declining birth rates are no longer confined to the western world. Birth-rate decline in large countries of the developing world is dramatic. China has a fertility rate of 1.5 and is the world's most populous country. India, with a fertility rate of 2.1, will soon overtake China as the world's most-populous nation. Brazil, the fifth most-populous country, has a fertility rate of 1.8.

Urbanisation

Why are fertility rates declining so dramatically in the developing world? *The Observer* article identifies urbanisation as one important driver. In 2007, for the first time ever, the majority of the global population lived in cities. Sixty-six per cent of the global population will live in cities within 30 years.

When women move from rural to city life, many things change that reduce birth rates. In the countryside a child can help by working on the land, but in a city a child is an economic liability. Also, cultural pressures to have more children recede in cities while access to media, schools and contraception increase.

Africa has the highest fertility rates in the world, accounting for most of the world's population growth. Unfortunately, Africa is also the world region presently worst-equipped to cater for burgeoning population numbers. But, birth rates are starting to fall, urbanisation is afoot and Africa already has a plentiful supply of young people, an essential resource to work a modern economy. Africa could well become an emerging China as this century progresses.

William Reville is an emeritus professor of biochemistry at UCC.

7 March 2019

World's population is projected to nearly stop growing by the end of the century

By Anthony Cilluffo and Neil G. Ruiz

For the first time in modern history, the world's population is expected to virtually stop growing by the end of this century, due in large part to falling global fertility rates, according to a Pew Research Center analysis of new data from the United Nations.

By 2100, the world's population is projected to reach approximately 10.9 billion, with annual growth of less than 0.1% – a steep decline from the current rate. Between 1950 and today, the world's population grew between 1% and 2% each year, with the number of people rising from 2.5 billion to more than 7.7 billion.

Here are 11 key takeaways from the UN's *World Population Prospects 2019*:

1 **The global fertility rate is expected to be 1.9 births per woman by 2100, down from 2.5 today.** The rate is projected to fall below the replacement fertility rate (2.1 births per woman) by 2070. The replacement fertility rate is the number of births per woman needed to maintain a population's size.

2 **The world's median age is expected to increase to 42 in 2100, up from the current 31 – and from 24 in 1950.** Between 2020 and 2100, the number of people aged 80 and older is expected to increase from 146 million to 881 million. Starting in 2073, there are projected to be more people ages 65 and older than under age 15 – the first time this will be the case. Contributing factors to the rise in the median age are the increase in life expectancy and falling fertility rates.

3 **Africa is the only world region projected to have strong population growth for the rest of this century.** Between 2020 and 2100, Africa's population is expected to increase from 1.3 billion to 4.3 billion. Projections show these gains will come mostly in sub-Saharan Africa, which is expected to more than triple in population by 2100. The regions that include the United States and Canada (Northern America) and Australia and New Zealand (Oceania) are projected to grow throughout the rest of the century, too, but at slower rates than Africa. (This analysis uses regional classifications from the UN and may differ from other Pew Research Center reports.)

4 **Europe and Latin America are both expected to have declining populations by 2100.** Europe's population is projected to peak at 748 million in 2021. The Latin America and Caribbean region is expected to surpass Europe in population by 2037 before peaking at 768 million in 2058.

5 **The population of Asia is expected to increase from 4.6 billion in 2020 to 5.3 billion in 2055, then start to decline.** China's population is expected to peak in 2031, while the populations of Japan and South Korea are projected to decline after 2020. India's population is expected to grow until 2059, when it will reach 1.7 billion. Meanwhile, Indonesia – the most populous country in Southeastern Asia – is projected to reach its peak population in 2067.

Global fertility is falling as the world is ageing

Number of live births per woman
(total fertility rate)

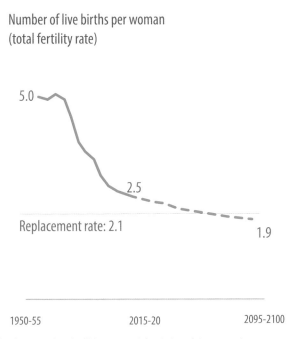

Median age of the world population

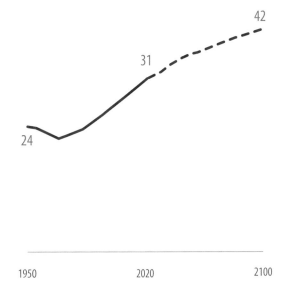

Note: The replacement rate is the number of births per woman required to maintain a population at a constant size.
Source: United Nations Department of Economic and Social Affairs, Population Division, 'World Population Prospects 2019'.

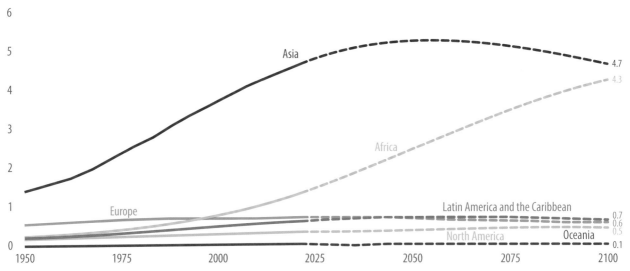

Population growth in Africa is projected to remain strong throughout this century

Population by region, in billions

Asia

Africa

Europe

Latin America and the Caribbean — 0.7
— 0.6
North America — 0.5
Oceania — 0.1

4.7
4.3

Note: Data labels show projected peak population for each region: Europe (2021), Asia (2055) and Latin America and the Caribbean (2058).
Source: United Nations Department of Economic and Social Affairs, Population Division, 'World Population Prospects 2019'.

6 **In the Northern America region, migration from the rest of the world is expected to be the primary driver of continued population growth.** The immigrant population in the United States is expected to see a net increase of 85 million over the next 80 years (2020 to 2100) according to the UN projections, roughly equal to the total of the next nine highest countries combined. In Canada, migration is likely to be a key driver of growth, as Canadian deaths are expected to outnumber births.

7 **Six countries are projected to account for more than half of the world's population growth through the end of this century, and five are in Africa.** The global population is expected to grow by about 3.1 billion people between 2020 and 2100. More than half of this increase is

projected to come from Nigeria, the Democratic Republic of the Congo, Tanzania, Ethiopia and Angola, along with one non-African country (Pakistan). Five African countries are projected to be in the world's top 10 countries by population by 2100.

8 **India is projected to surpass China as the world's most-populous country by 2027.** Meanwhile, Nigeria will surpass the US as the third-largest country in the world in 2047, according to the projections.

9 **Between 2020 and 2100, 90 countries are expected to lose population.** Two-thirds of all countries and territories in Europe (32 of 48) are expected to lose population by 2100. In Latin America and the Caribbean,

By 2100, five of the world's ten largest countries are projected to be in Africa
Countries with largest population, in millions

1950		2020		2100	
China	554	China	1,439	India	1,450
India	376	India	1,380	China	1,065
US	159	US	331	Nigeria	733
Russia	103	Indonesia	274	US	434
Japan	83	Pakistan	221	Pakistan	403
Germany	70	Brazil	213	D.R. Congo	362
Indonesia	70	Nigeria	206	Indonesia	321
Brazil	54	Bangladesh	165	Ethiopia	294
UK	51	Russia	146	Tanzania	286
Italy	47	Mexico	129	Egypt	225

Note: Countries are based on current borders. In this data source, China does not include Hong Kong, Macau or Taiwan
Source: United Nations Department of Economic and Social Affairs, Population Division, 'World Population Prospects 2019'.

By 2100, half of babies born worldwide are expected to be born in Africa

% of babies born, by region

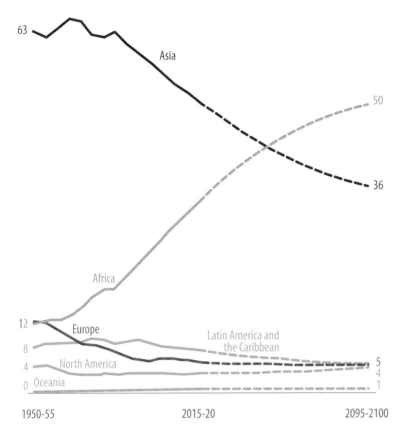

Source: United Nations Department of Economic and Social Affairs, Population Division, 'World Population Prospects 2019'.

in Nigeria is projected to exceed those in China by 2070.

Meanwhile, roughly a third of the world's babies are projected to be born in Asia by the end of this century, down from about half today and from a peak of 65% in the 1965–70 period.

11 **The Latin America and Caribbean region is expected to have the oldest population of any world region by 2100, a reversal from the 20th century.** In 1950, the region's median age was just 20 years. That figure is projected to more than double to 49 years by 2100.

This pattern is evident when looking at individual countries in the region. For example, in 2020, the median ages of Brazil (33), Argentina (32) and Mexico (29) are all expected to be lower than the median age in the US (38). However, by 2100, all three of these Latin American nations are projected to be older than the US The median age will be 51 in Brazil, 49 in Mexico and 47 in Argentina, compared with a median age of 45 in the US Colombia is expected to undergo a particularly stark transition, with its median age more than tripling between 1965 and 2100 – from 16 to 52.

Japan is projected to have the highest median age of any country in the world in 2020, at 48 years old. Japan's median age is expected to continue to rise until it peaks at 55 in 2065. It is expected to be lower in 2100 (54). By that time, the country with the highest median age is expected to be Albania, with a median age of 61.

17 June 2019

www.pewresearch.org

half of the region's 50 countries' populations are expected to shrink. Between 1950 and 2020, by contrast, only six countries in the world lost population, due to much higher fertility rates and a relatively younger population in past decades.

10 **Africa is projected to overtake Asia in births by 2060.** Half of babies born worldwide are expected to be born in Africa by 2100, up from three-in-ten today. Nigeria is expected to have 864 million births between 2020 and 2100, the most of any African country. The number of births

What goes up: are predictions of a population crisis wrong?

Changing fertility rates challenge dystopian visions and UN projections about the future of our overcrowded planet

By Darrell Bricker and John Ibbitson

She is a well-educated, professional woman, working in an office tower in central Nairobi, Kenya. Because of her status and education, the price required to marry her is bound to be high. Although dowries are often now paid in cash, she expects hers will be paid in the traditional method of cows and goats, and that the wedding will take place in the village she came from.

'I'm a traditional girl,' she explains.

It could take a long time for any suitor to accumulate the capital needed to pay – or at least down-pay – her dowry. She's fine with that.

'We [women] are getting married later,' one of her colleagues explains. 'We want an education, job security, and a nice place to live… This also means that we can't have as many kids, even if we want them.'

These remarks offer a window on one of the most compelling questions of our time: how many people will fill the Earth? The United Nations Population Division projects that numbers will swell to more than 11 billion by the end of this century, almost four billion more than are alive today. Where will they live? How will we feed them? How many more of us can our fragile planet withstand?

But a growing body of opinion believes the UN is wrong. We will not reach 11 billion by 2100. Instead, the human population will top out at somewhere between eight and nine billion around the middle of the century, and then begin to decline.

Jørgen Randers, a Norwegian academic who decades ago warned of a potential global catastrophe caused by overpopulation, has changed his mind. 'The world population will never reach nine billion people,' he now believes. 'It will peak at eight billion in 2040, and then decline.'

Similarly, Prof. Wolfgang Lutz and his fellow demographers at Vienna's International Institute for Applied Systems Analysis predict the human population will stabilise by mid-century and then start to go down.

A Deutsche Bank report has the planetary population peaking at 8.7 billion in 2055 and then declining to 8 billion by century's end.

The UN discounts the claims of these experts, relying on the authority of experience. 'We imagine that countries that currently have higher levels of fertility and lower levels of life expectancy will make progress in the future in a similar manner, at a similar speed, to what was experienced by countries in the past,' John Wilmoth, director of the UN Population Division, says. 'It's all grounded in past experience.'

But the dissident demographers think this is wrong, primarily because the UN is failing to account for an accelerating decline in fertility as a result of urbanisation. In 2007, for the first time in human history, the majority of people in the world lived in cities. Today, it's 55%. In three decades, it will be two-thirds.

A lot happens when people move from the countryside into the city. First, a child changes from being an asset – another pair of shoulders to work in the fields – to a burden – another mouth to feed.

Even more important, a woman who moves to a city has greater access to media, to schools, to other women. She demands greater autonomy. And many women who are able to exercise control over their own bodies decide to have fewer children.

'The brain is the most important reproductive organ,' Lutz asserts. 'Once a woman is socialised to have an education and a career, she is socialised to have a smaller family. There's no going back.'

Religious and familial pressures to settle down and make babies also recede in the city; friends and co-workers, who are largely indifferent to one another's reproductive choices, become more important.

Already, almost two dozen countries are getting smaller every year, from Poland to Cuba to Japan, which lost almost 450,000 people in 2018. In these countries, women have fewer than the 2.1 babies that they must produce, on average, for a population to remain stable. The population decline would be even steeper were it not for steadily increasing life expectancy.

The fertility rate in the UK is 1.7. Most population growth in the UK today is the result of international immigration, according to the Office of National Statistics. Without immigrants, Great Britain would eventually enter an era of population decline.

More old people and fewer young people place an increased strain on society's ability to generate the wealth and taxes needed to fund, among other things, healthcare for the old.

The really big news, however, is found in the large countries of the developing world, where the great majority of people live. There, declines in birth rates have been simply astonishing. China, the world's largest country, has a fertility rate of 1.5, lower than Britain's. India, soon to overtake China

> *"As people move to cities, marginal farmland reverts to bush, a natural carbon sink and a boon to wildlife"*

as the world's most populous nation, is at the replacement rate of 2.1 and falling. Brazil, the fifth most populous country, has a fertility rate of 1.8.

Africa remains the cradle of overpopulation, with fertility rates far above replacement. If the human population truly is heading towards 11 billion people, as the UN predicts, then the African story in this century will be grim; the continent will remain largely poor and rural. Women will be forced to have child after child, swelling the numbers of humanity in the one place on Earth that can least easily sustain them.

But this is far too pessimistic a prognosis. Parts of Africa are making great strides in empowering women and reducing the number of children they have. Kenya is one example, though not the only one.

The horrific attack by the Islamist terrorist group al-Shabaab on a hotel and business complex earlier this month brought home once again the challenges facing this sub-Saharan nation of 50 million.

Only about a quarter of its people earn a salary from either a private- or public-sector employer, which is the very definition of a modern workforce. Half the population doesn't believe it gets enough to eat and about a third reports sometimes going to bed hungry.

On the other hand, over 75% of the population have mobile device subscriptions. In the past three decades, the country's urban population has more than doubled to 32%. And as it urbanises, Kenya's fertility rate plummets: from eight in 1960, according to World Bank figures, to 3.4 today, according to a new study of global fertility rates published last November in *The Lancet*.

Almost as many girls as boys sat last year for the exams that permit students to graduate from primary school (at the age of 14, after eight years of formal education). On average, the girls scored better.

Many Kenyan women live two lives at the same time. The first is immemorial, agricultural, subsistent and patriarchal. However, in her back pocket she has a mobile phone. And though she hasn't told her parents yet, she's planning to move to the city.

Elsewhere the fertility rate figures are less encouraging: Niger, 7; Mali, 6; Nigeria, 5. But even there, changes are happening: Nigeria's fertility rate was almost seven in 1980.

Women make up 61% of the members of Rwanda's parliament, the highest proportion of any government. The fertility rate in that country has plummeted from eight to four in the past 30 years. Sub-Saharan Africa is the fastest urbanising part of the world, with annual urban population increases of 4%, twice the global average.

With any luck, Africa in this century will feature urbanisation, better-educated girls and women, and falling fertility. Not everywhere, and not all at once, but in more places than not, and sooner rather than later.

From Malthusian predictions at global conferences to the latest dystopian offering from Hollywood, pessimists predict a future of overcrowding, scarcity, conflict and possible collapse. But the premise is probably false. We need to prepare, not for the consequences of a population boom, but a population bust. A child born this decade will probably reach middle age in a world where population growth has stalled, and may already have begun to shrink. There could be much about this world to admire. It may be cleaner, safer, quieter. Urbanisation produces a marked decrease in carbon emissions per person – people using public transport, for example, rather than travelling by car – and as people move to the city, marginal farmland reverts to bush, a natural carbon sink and a boon to wildlife.

Economically, however, things could be more challenging, as societies struggle to grow with fewer young workers and taxpayers. Automation will help, but robots don't buy refrigerators or a smart dress for the office party. Consumption remains the bedrock of any economy.

Population decline is not a good thing or a bad thing. But it is a big thing. It's time to look it in the eye.

27 January 2019

Europe population 2020

Europe is a subcontinent that comprises the westernmost peninsula of Eurasia. It's usually divided from Asia by the watershed divides of the Ural River, the Caspian and Black Seas, the Caucasus and Ural Mountains and waterways that connect the Black and Aegean Seas together. The continent's estimated 2016 population is over 738 million.

Europe is the second-smallest continent by surface area and covers 10.18 million square kilometres (3.93 million square miles), or 2% of the Earth's surface and 6.8% of the world's land area. There are approximately 50 countries in Europe. The largest by size is Russia with 40% of the continent, and Vatican City is the smallest.

Europe is the third most populous continent behind Asia and Africa. Its population in 2016 is estimated at 738 million, which accounts for 11% of the world's population. The continent is currently growing at a rate of 0.3%. Europe has been in a decline for some time and its population is aging rapidly in most countries.

Most populous countries

By far the most populous country in Europe is Russia, which is actually located in both Europe and Asia. Russia's population of 143 million is almost equal to the combined populations of the second and third most populous countries on the continent.

Russia is a very interesting situation, as its population is very hard to determine with Russian and CIA estimates varying by three million. The country is also very representative of all of Europe with a rapidly declining population growth and an aging population.

Least populous countries

The least populous country in Europe is Vatican City with just over 800 residents. It's also the smallest internationally recognised independent state in the world, both in area and population. Vatican City is a landlocked city-state with a territory consisting of a walled enclave within Rome, Italy. Vatican City is ruled by the Pope and it's the sovereign territory of the Holy See.

Comparison to other continents

Europe is the second-smallest continent by surface area but the third most populous after Asia and Africa. The population density of Europe as a whole is 143 people per square mile (compared to Asia's 203/square mile), which makes it the second most densely populated continent.

The top 10 most populous countries in Europe are:

Russia (143.45 million)*

Germany (81.4 million)*

France (66.4 million)

United Kingdom (65.08 million)

Italy (60.93 million)*

Spain (46.42 million)*

Ukraine (42.85 million)*

Poland (38.49 million)*

Romania (19.82 million)*

Kazakhstan (17.54 million)

*countries with a declining population.

The 10 least populous countries (not territories) in Europe are:

Vatican City (800)

San Marino (33,000)

Monaco (37,000)

Liechtenstein (37,000)

Andorra (78,000)

Iceland (331,000)

Malta (425,000)

Luxembourg (570,000)

Montenegro (620,000)

Cyprus (876,000)

Europe is leading the world in countries with declining population growth and an aging population, but this problem is one that affects most developed countries at some point.

Europe population growth

It's projected that Europe will lose 30 million people of working age by 2050, while the number of people in their 80s and 90s will rise dramatically. This *New York Times* article is an interesting read for learning more about Europe's declining population and fertility rates. Most European countries are dealing with the effects of an aging population, including fertility rates below replacement level as fewer women have children in favour of a career. The population of the European Union (EU) is now expected to peak in 2040 with the sharpest population declines in Romania and Germany (-19%), Bulgaria (-27%), Latvia (-26%) and Lithuania (-20%).

Europe's largest country, Russia, is expected to drop from today's 143 million to just 107 million by 2050.

12 May 2019

www.worldpopulationreview.com

How many people live in Europe?

747,636,026*

Percentage of world population

9.96%

Density
(persons/square km)

33.78

* This is based on United Nation estimates and is correct at time of press

Depopulation instead of overpopulation

Every now and then, the somewhat controversial scenario of depopulation instead of overpopulation enters the stage of future demographic trends. Like overpopulation, depopulation would have widespread consequences for the environment, the labour market and social and cultural practices. In the recent book *Empty Planet*, the thought that we might have to deal with depopulation in the future popped up again: the global population, now 7.5 billon, will decline rapidly later this century after peaking below 9 billion – rather than the 11 billion that is predicted by the United Nations. Why does this scenario of depopulation keep coming back, and is it becoming more realistic?

Our observations

◆ According to the United Nations (UN), the world population will grow from 7.6 billion today to 2 billion by 2100. It is expected that more than half of global population growth until 2050 will occur in Africa, with Niger topping the list at 7.153 children per woman, followed by Somalia at 6.123 children per woman. The lowest-fertility countries now include all countries in Europe and Northern America, and many countries in Asia (e.g. Japan, Taiwan and Singapore) and Latin America (e.g. Mexico and Brazil).

◆ The new book *Empty Planet: The Shock of Global Population Decline* foresees global population peaking at 9 billion by 2060 and predicts that by 2100, it will have shrunk to 7 billion, after which the decline will continue. The main reasons for this decline are urbanisation and the empowerment (mostly by education) of women.

The authors, Canadian journalist John Ibbitson and political scientist Darrell Bricker, claim that 'the great defining event of the twenty-first century will occur in three decades, give or take, when the global population starts to decline. Once that decline begins, it will never end.'

◆ In the past two decades, several theories on population decline have appeared. For example, Nicholas Eberstadt published the article *Too few people?* arguing that 'global population will peak in 2040 and then start a headlong dive'; Fred Pearce argued in his book *The Coming Population Crash: and Our Planet's Surprising Future* that the global trend to empower women through education and equal rights causes lower birth rates and by 2040, the world's population will be declining for the first time since the Black Death reduced the world's population from an estimated 450 million down to 350–375 million in the 14th century.

◆ Whether we're facing a decline or growth of the global population has great impact on our forecast of and, therefore, policy on food production, climate change, the future of work, healthcare, pensions, (im)migration, economic growth and so on. Both prospects come with their own set of positive and negative consequences. Population decline, for example, is thought to be a good thing for the planet, because human activities will be less of a burden, whereas slower economic growth or ageing populations are negative consequences that population growth doesn't have.

Connecting the dots

In *An Essay on the Principle of Population*, published in 1798, Thomas Malthus painted a dystopic picture of a future in which population would increase geometrically, doubling every 25 years, without food production being able to keep up. This would result in worldwide famine and starvation, called 'the Malthusian trap'. He concluded that birthrates had to be controlled in order to prevent a humanitarian disaster. This was a major stimulus for countries to install population controllers, as shown by mass US-funded family planning programmes, Iran's birth control policy, India pressuring its citizens to get sterilised, and China introducing its one-child policy, which led to forced abortions. Later on, many others expressed the same concern for overpopulation and its disastrous consequences, such as Al Gore and the Club of Rome.

However, counter-predictions on demographic trends were also introduced. In 1921, for example, philosopher Oswald Spengler argued in *The Decline of the West* that every civilisation will eventually decline at its peak of intelligence, referring to a point in its history at which a culture has flourished and reached great welfare. At this time, cultural phenomena such as urbanisation and feminism take flight and depopulation will start. The decline of population based on these two factors is reintroduced by, for example, Eberstadt and Pearce. Rural societies, for example, consider children an asset: they are very cheap land workers and later on, they can take care of their parents when they get old. In the city, however, children cannot fulfil such a role. Instead they put a heavy burden on households and hinder (especially) women in pursuing a career. What is more, the empowerment of women includes education in the first years of fertility, which causes a delay in having children, which often leads to not having them at all. Furthermore, after education, women choose to have fewer children in order to pursue a career or other ambitions, and if having children is in the way of their life ambitions, they will choose not to become a mum at all.

In their calculations on global population growth rates, the UN considers fertility, migration, and death rates. The main argument in *Empty Planet* that aims to make the scenario of a global depopulation more plausible at this point in time, is that urbanisation and the empowerment of women have a huge impact on population rates. Furthermore, they claim the expansion of education for women and urbanisation are currently happening fastest in developing countries. The UN therefore erroneously assumes that Africa will stagnate in rural poverty for the rest of the century. Moreover, the immense speed of dropping fertility rates due to these factors has already been demonstrated in other areas. In the Philippines (a country in which urbanisation has been happening relatively fast), for example, fertility rates dropped from 3.7 in 2003 to 2.7 in 2018. Ibbitson points out that historically, such a change in fertility rates took shape much more slowly in countries such as the US, namely from about 1800 to the end of the Baby Boom.

The process of urbanisation originated more than two centuries ago, but the next urbanisation wave might indeed be of unprecedented scale and pace, making a scenario of depopulation more plausible in current times. Furthermore, Africa, which is thought of as the biggest contributor to population growth by the UN, has successfully benefited from a number of cases of 'leapfrogging' technology, such as mobile phones over land line connections, access to mobile banking through services such as M-Pesa in Kenya and Tanzania. According to GSMA Intelligence, smartphone adoption in Africa will rise from 37% in 2017 to 67% by 2025. Smartphone adoption could be a huge impulse for e-learning and thereby raise the level of education in many African countries by solving pressing problems such as teacher shortage, lack of curriculum, etc. The empowerment of women in Africa could therefore take flight as well, since many more girls will be educated partly during their first years of fertility and might then develop other ambitions than motherhood alone.

The two factors, urbanisation and the empowerment of women, already pointed out by Spengler at the beginning of the former century, have indeed proven to cause depopulation over time in certain regions. The fact that they are currently gaining momentum on a global scale makes the scenario of depopulation more plausible than before.

Implications

◆ According to the authors of *Empty Planet*, depopulation will have positive effects on the environment, since it means there will be less people to burden our planet. However, as logical as this argumentation might seem, the opposite could be the case as well. For, if depopulation also means that more people will be wealthier, the environment might suffer from depopulation when current dynamics remain unchanged: the richest 10% of people now produce half of Earth's climate-harming fossil-fuel emissions, while the poorest half contribute a mere 10%.

◆ Forecasts of population rates will remain rather uncertain due to the many factors that can influence their course. As we wrote before, other factors such as life expectancy or religious or political views on reproduction can influence the fertility rates of a country as well. The effects of population growth or decline are uncertain too. Some even argue that both scenarios could equally be used as a positive or negative argument for wealth, environment or innovation.

22 February 2019

Our population is heading towards ten billion - and Chris Packham thinks we might need a one-child policy to save the world

We are putting a strain on the planet, but is the BBC presenter of 7.7 Billion People and Counting right to suggest we have fewer kids?

By Sophie Morris

It is the ethical dilemma that dare not speak its name, or even whisper it. But Chris Packham, admittedly not known for piping down, has decided enough is enough. The stakes, the survival of our species and of our planet, are too high.

The big issue? Population control. And Packham's mission, with a one-off BBC programme broadcast next week, is to make having children as uncool as eating meat or drinking from a disposable cup. If you do have to reproduce, please stick to one.

The naturalist and broadcaster knows it will cause a stir. That's his intention. 'I'm not here to make friends,' he told reporters after a preview screening of *7.7 Billion People and Counting* last month. 'I'm here to make a difference... My duty is to pull people's heads out of the sand.'

During Packham's lifetime of 58 years, the population of the world has doubled. In Sir David Attenborough's 93 years, it has tripled. There were only five million people on the planet 10,000 years ago. Today, there are around 7.7 billion humans walking the Earth.

'Sphere of destruction'

The United Nations predicts that our numbers will rise to almost ten billion by 2050. They will need more space. They will need more to eat, resulting in more land being deforested for farms, which will need more water and risk exhausting soil. And they will need more energy, when we need to radically reduce and eliminate net carbon emissions. Can our planet sustain such numbers? If not, can anything be done about it?

Packham calls the triangle of climate change, biodiversity loss and population growth a 'sphere of destruction'. But where the first two are accepted causes of planetary devastation, and our overconsumption of meat and plastic is a fixture on the news agenda, discussing the birth rate is as risky as bringing up Brexit at a family meal.

His view is shared by the leading gerontologist Professor Sarah Harper, a founder of the Oxford Institute of Population Ageing. 'We're definitely at a turning point,' she agrees. 'The next two or three decades are going to be crucial.'

Coupled with birth rate is the spectre of our ageing population. 'We're so good at saving lives,' Packham says in the documentary, after introducing his 86-year-old father – who in previous centuries would have died from the heart attack he suffered, but is alive thanks to modern medicine. 'We haven't been so good at thinking about what to do because we've saved them.'

Despite rapid drops in the birth rate of many developed nations, globally the rate is still rising. Along with Sir David, Dame Jane Goodall and James Lovelock, Packham is a patron of the controversial charity Population Matters, which campaigns for a sustainable number of humans to live in harmony with other species and our environment.

Are you starting to feel uncomfortable? As Sir David tells Packham in the programme: 'It's very difficult to talk about because the right to have children is one of the most precious rights that people have.'

And given that the biggest increases in population are happening in the developing world, some critics say that trying to stop it is racist – though Packham has angrily rejected this argument as 'mis-informed'.

Social issues

On the one hand fears about population control can be smartly dismissed as Malthusian scare-mongering. The 18th century economist Thomas Malthus predicted a soaring population, but wrongly yoked it to unavoidable poverty, failing to foresee rising living standards, disease prevention and contraception.

On the other, China's one-child policy and India's forced sterilisation programme in the 1970s are brutal examples of population control. These models failed, says Packham – but other countries, including South Korea, Thailand and Iran, have operated successful birth control policies. So successful that all three nations, along with many others, have since tried to boost their declining populations to revitalise their economies with a younger workforce. They have all struggled.

In England and Wales the birth rate hit a record low of 1.7 per woman in 2018. In Africa, that figure is four – high but falling. In his programme, Packham visits Nigeria's largest city Lagos, which has 21 million inhabitants and a birth rate of five. Home to 200 million people, Nigeria is the most populous country in Africa, and at current rates its citizenship will double by 2050.

Globally the birth rate is 2.4, and we only need to lower the birth rate to 2.1 to stabilise population growth. How could this be done? 'If you were to rub a lamp and give me a wish,' says Packham, 'it would be the immediate emancipation of women all over the planet. In every example looked at, it significantly reduced the birth rate and improved the quality of life for both the woman and the family.'

Professor Danny Dorling is a social geographer at the University of Oxford. He explains that tiny changes in the number of births have huge impacts later. 'What is happening right now,' he says, 'is the first ever slowdown of human population in the history of our species not due to a disaster. Contraception helped, because given the choice, women would rather have fewer children to look after. The vast majority of women do not want a large family.'

They don't? I read *Cheaper by the Dozen* over and over as a child. I had two older sisters already, but the idea of a house bursting with siblings was the most exciting existence I could imagine. You'd never be short of friends. Every weekday meal would be a celebration. Think of the parties!

While not fantasy, the novel by brother and sister Frank Bunker Gilbreth Jr and Ernestine Gilbreth Carey was so far-fetched you couldn't make it up, and was indeed based on the authors' lives growing up in a family of 12 children. But the jolly-hockey-sticks, make-do-and-mend, all-rubbing-along-nicely-together Gilbreth household is as far from contemporary standards as any.

When, in 2018, my baby became a toddler and people started asking when I was having a second, my feelings began to align with Dorling's. I am not capable of sustaining a large family, emotionally or financially. Forget a dozen, I'm not sure I'm capable of sustaining more than one.

I bought all the books on raising an only child that I could find. There are two by Susan Newman which are practical, heartening and confidently debunk those myths of weird, spoilt, unsociable, slow to develop and lonely souls.

The Only Child by Jill Pitkeathley and David Emerson deals with the 'legacy of burdens' you bestow upon your child by not providing siblings. But my favourite is by New York journalist Lauren Sandler, an only child herself. In *One and Only*, she guides readers through the reality of having more than one child for a working woman in the 21st century.

Society's view of an ideal family hasn't caught up with the personal and professional needs of emancipated women. Hopefully the future will reveal more positive ways of having one child, or being childless. But we need to get a bloody move on.

BirthStrikers go much further. They are a group of women who have vowed not to have children until significant progress has been made on climate change. You see, this isn't only about the parents or the planet, it's about the sort of world we're bringing children into. Will we see a rise in anti-natalists, such as the odd case of Raphael Samuel, the Indian man suing his parents for giving birth to him?

Lifestyle changes

If our population continues to grow, our world might survive but our lifestyles will suffer. To illustrate this, Packham visits São Paulo where Maria lives in an apartment with her two sons. Last year she clubbed together with other residents in her block for a private well to be dug. Constructing a private water source is becoming commonplace in the Brazilian megacity, where there are frequent shortages. São Paulo has over 12 million residents; 13,000 of them built their own wells last year.

It is predicted that within 25 years, England could face water shortages – and might need supplies from Scotland to cope.

Packham is frequently portrayed as a misanthrope. He admits he often doesn't hold the human species in high regard. He doesn't have his own children but is close to his 24-year-old stepdaughter. Arguably he's taking up more than his fair share of space, living alone with his dogs in a large cottage surrounded by woodland. He likes to think of himself as someone who doesn't need much stuff, then confesses to owning ten vacuum cleaners.

Is having one child the solution to climate change? In his recent book *SOS: Simple Actions that Make a Difference*, climate change researcher Seth Wynne found that only having one child reduces your cumulative carbon emissions by a whopping 58.6 tonnes a year. For context: living car free for a year saves 2.4 tonnes.

However, Professor Corey Bradshaw of Australia's Flinders University modelled what would happen if the global fertility rate dropped from 2.4 to 2 tomorrow: the population trajectory would reduce by about 50 per cent by 2100, but we'd only get a 7 per cent decline in total emissions, because most come from developed nations where the rate is already low. If the birth rate goes down but everyone consumes like the average Brit, we'd need nearly two more Earths.

Packham believes we need to look at 'measuring, understanding, and ultimately controlling' global population growth, but admits: 'There is no simple solution.' That's true, unless we all join the Voluntary Human Extinction Movement (yes, they are a thing). Lots of families will wonder where this leaves them. I'm confident there's no evidence that only children are disadvantaged in any way, but that doesn't assuage my urge to give my daughter siblings. Could anyone who's seen *Little Women* this month disagree?

My husband Ben has been ready to get the snip for environmental reasons for months, though I joke that we might need his swimmers after the Third World War.

I agree with Packham – the conversation around population control should be amplified – and yet I feel less guilty about having a child than I did before. Education and female emancipation is the way to change things. Let's get to it.

14 January 2020

Meet the 'birth strikers', who aren't having children for the sake of the planet

By Gareth Rubin

How selfish is having children? Without doubt, our world is oversubscribed, and thinkers including Sir David Attenborough have highlighted population growth as one of the gravest threats to the future of our planet.

Population has doubled in the last half-century, rocketing from 3.61 billion to 7.3 billion today, and bringing children into this world means taking the food out of others' mouths, putting more pressure on natural resources, and potentially sentencing those children to a life of uncertainty and hunger.

Last week, swathes of London and parts of the rail network were brought to a standstill by protesters from the radical environmentalist group Extinction Rebellion, who argue the danger to future generations cannot be ignored. Now, increasing numbers of adults are questioning not only whether having children is something they want to do, but also if it's something that it's right to do.

I am 43, and many of my generation have made the leap into parenthood in the past few years – happily sharing scan photos, scoping out buggies and arguing in the baby section at Ikea. For them, altruistic concerns for the environment or the danger of their children being born into a harsh world were dwarfed by a biological need to reproduce, alongside the joy they would feel bringing up a son or daughter.

I have long taken a different view – I have decided I do not want children, due to a combination of existential fears about what will happen to our society over the 100-year life-span of any child of mine, mixed with a long-standing belief that I am largely unsuited for fatherhood.

My friend Anusha, a 28-year-old retail analyst, is another 'birth striker', deciding when she was about 21 that she didn't want to have children. 'At the time lots of friends and family told me that as I got older, the biological clock would start ticking,' she recalls.

'But actually the opposite has happened. The older I've got the more my decision had solidified. There are now a lot of wider issues that I'm passionate about in terms of the planet and climate change that have confirmed that decision for me. Beyond not eating meat, recycling, using public transport, the number one thing that you can do for the planet is not reproduce.'

Anna Hughes, a cycling instructor and author, agrees. 'It's inescapable that having kids... creates a resource-consuming person,' she says, adding that if she were to fall pregnant, 'I would have an abortion.'

Interest in halting procreation for the sake of the planet is growing. Population Matters, a charity that addresses the effect of population size on the environment, has seen their online traffic and social media following soar, with a Facebook post on going child-free reaching 4 million people.

The charity maintains that 'smaller families mean better lives for all,' and cites Thailand, a country which reduced its fertility rate by nearly 75 percent over two generations with a targeted family planning drive, as a model we should be following.

The BBC is currently exploring the debate over slowing population growth via its Blue Planet Live tour and an upcoming series of documentaries, *Protecting Our Planet*. 'The single most important thing to deal with is population growth. We're just simply running out of resources,' said Chris Packham, who presents one of the films. 'Do you want to bring something you will cherish and love and value into a world where they might no longer survive?'

> 'The single most important thing to deal with is population growth. We're just simply running out of resources.'
>
> Chris Packham

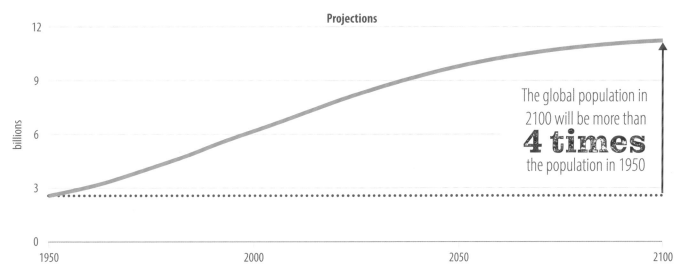

Global population past and projected

Projections

The global population in 2100 will be more than **4 times** the population in 1950

Source: UN World Population Prospects

The dilemma has not been lost on my friend Kate, 36. Since the birth of her first child, Raph, four months ago, she has become more eco-conscious. 'I'm worried about his future and 80 years down the line is looking pretty bleak, so the issue of overpopulation would definitely make me think twice about having another.' As such, adoption has become a consideration in answering a possible future desire to reproduce, she says – and, 'if I do have another child, I would want to raise two individuals who were equipped and wanted to do their best for the planet'.

Overpopulation leads to severe economic problems too, says, Suzanne, 28, who works in marketing and has also chosen not to have children. 'I just don't feel that the world needs more people,' she says. 'The way cities are expanding so rapidly produces cheap labour and keeps wages down, and that means competition for resources. It's not a world in which I would envision wanting to raise children... I don't want to add to the problem.'

Sometimes, it has been uncomfortable explaining her decision. 'I'm not in a relationship right now, but it's something I'm aware of when those questions come up – and some men have been put off by it. It's always a difficult conversation to have.'

I know this all too well – over the years my zero-child policy undoubtedly ended relationships. After a few dates, we would have the conversation and I would explain that children just weren't part of my life plan. Usually we would go out a few more – subdued – times while she thought it over, but then more often than not she would say that forgoing a family would be too hard, and it would be best if we left things.

Of course, emotional urges to have a child may always overtake environmental ones and, over the years, friends and family have tried valiantly to change my mind with the usual arguments: 'Children will look after you when you're old', 'they keep you young', 'you'll have fun with them'. When I told my mother I was sure I didn't want them she was disappointed, but at least my brother had reproduced so that took some of the heat off me. It didn't stop her from occasionally holding up pictures of babies in magazines in a silent attempt to persuade me otherwise, though.

I am now in a relationship with a 37-year-old woman and, for the first time, find myself beginning to waver ever so slightly from my decision. I can't say what caused it, but perhaps I have just reached the point at which a visceral urge trumps a thought-out argument – even one I've maintained for decades. From time to time, I'll see a father with his son, talking about castles or Gothic literature or spies, and something inside me kicks. It says I should be there too, making up explanations for how birds stay in the air.

My position hasn't entirely reversed, but I suppose mine and my girlfriend's respective ages mean that if we're going to do it, we had better get on with it. She knows that I used to be firmly against having offspring, and the vestiges of that preference can be a worry for both of us: what if it turns out in the end that I'm not cut out to be a father after all? It's a risk. And I haven't told friends or family that I may renege on my birth striker status – it seems too personal, somehow, as if I'm asking for approbation. I'm going to just let it come out if and when the issue arises.

Yes, the intellectual case against having children, the worries about their future on an overpopulated planet and my ability to provide well for them, are still there. Yet times change, and maybe I have, too.

21 April 2019

Key Facts

- In mid-2018, the population of the UK reached an estimated 66.4 million. (page 1)

- In 2018, the UK experienced a natural change of 115,000 with 731,000 live births and 616,000 deaths – the lowest level of natural change since 2003. (page 2)

- 2018 shows that the number of live births was the lowest recorded since 2005 and the birth rate was the lowest ever recorded (11.1 live births per 1,000 total population). (page 2)

- In 2018, about 85.7% of the UK population were UK-born and about 90.7% were British nationals – down from about 88.9% and 93.1%, respectively, in 2008. (page 4)

- By 2050, it is projected that one in four people in the UK will be aged 65 years and over. (page 4)

- Life expectancy at birth did not improve in 2015 to 2017, when compared with 2014 to 2016 life expectancy, and remained at 79.2 years for males and 82.9 years for females. (page 5)

- The UK population is set to increase by 3 million within the next 10 years and pass the 70 million mark in the early 2030s. (page 6)

- England's population is anticipated to grow faster than the other UK nations, increasing by 5 per cent between 2018 and 2028. (page 6)

- In 2018, the number of live births fell from 11.6 per 1,000 people to 11.1, the lowest since records started in 1938. (page 7)

- The most common age of motherhood declined from about 25 in the post-war period, to around 22 in the early 1970s, and now stands at about 31 years of age. (page 9)

- Having one fewer child reduces a parent's carbon footprint by 58 tonnes of CO_2 a year. (page 10)

- The UK's average age has been rising steadily, from 36 in 1975 to 40 today. (page 12)

- In 2017, the percentage of the population aged 85 years and over was 2.7 times greater than it was in 1971.(page 13)

- In 2016, UK life expectancy at birth was above the European Union (EU) average for males, but below the EU average for females. (page 13)

- A child born between 2016 and 2018 can expect to live to 79.3 if they are male and 82.9 if they are female. (page 18)

- In 2019 the planet has 7.7 billion inhabitants. (page 19)

- It is estimated that about 81 million people add to the world's population annually. (page 22)

- Rainforests originally covered 14% of the entire earth's surface. Today, rainforest only cover about 6% of the earth's surface. (page 22)

- One in two people wrongly believes that there are sufficient natural resources for all humans to live like those in rich countries. (page 24)

- Six in ten people consider the world to be more dangerous in 2018 than two years ago. (page 24)

- The proportion of people who consider population growth a global catastrophic risk has decreased from 80% in 2017 to 70% today and only 23% now believe the issue warrants urgent action, compared to a third of respondents in 2017.(page 24)

- UK millennials were more likely to think that the consequences of population growth will be positive (16% vs 1% of baby boomers). (page 24)

- In order for a human population to maintain its numbers, each woman must bear, on average, 2.1 children. If the birth rate exceeds 2.1, population numbers increase; if it is less than 2.1, population numbers decline. (page 26)

- India, with a fertility rate of 2.1, will soon overtake China as the world's most populous nation. (page 26)

- In 2007, for the first time ever, the majority of the global population lived in cities. (page 26)

- By 2100, the world's population is projected to reach approximately 10.9 billion. (page 27)

- Europe's population is projected to peak at 748 million in 2021. (page 27)

- Japan is projected to have the highest median age of any country in the world in 2020, at 48 years old. (page 29)

- A Deutsche Bank report has the planetary population peaking at 8.7 billion in 2055 and then declining to 8 billion by century's end. (page 30)

- Kenya's fertility rate has plummeted from 8 in 1960, to 3.4 today. (page 31)

- Russsia is the most populous country in Europe. It has a population of 143 million, which is almost equal to the combined populations of the 2nd and 3rd most populous countries in Europe. (page 32)

- The least populous country in Europe is Vatican City with just over 800 residents. (page 32)

- It's projected that Europe will lose 30 million people of working age by 2050, while the number of people in their 80s and 90s will rise dramatically. (page 33)

- The Black Death reduced the world's population from an estimated 450 million down to 350–375 million in the 14th century. (page 34)

Ageing population

A population whose average age is rising. This can be caused by increased life expectancy, for example following significant medical advances, or by falling birth rates, for example due to the introduction of contraception. However, the higher the proportion of older people within a population, the lower the birth rate will become due to there being fewer people of childbearing age.

Birth rate

The number of live births within a population over a given period of time, often expressed as the number of births per 1,000 of the population.

Death rate

The number of deaths within a population over a given period of time, often expressed as number of deaths per 1,000 of the population.

Demographic changes (ageing population/grey population)

Demographics refer to the structure of a population. We are currently experiencing an increase in our ageing population. People are living longer thanks to advancements in medical treatment and care. Soon, the world will have more older people than children. This means that the need for long-term care is rising.

Demographics

Statistical characteristics of a population: for example, age, race or employment status.

Depopulation

The substantial decline or reduction in the population of an area.

Infant mortality rate

The number of infant deaths (infants are usually defined as one year old or younger) per 1,000 live births of the population.

LIfe expectancy

The average period that a person may be expected to live.

Migration

To migrate is to move from one's home country and settle in another.

Natural change

Natural change is the number of births minus the number of deaths.

Overpopulation

Overpopulation is when an area's population exceeds the capacity of the environment to support it to an acceptable standard of living.

Population growth

An increase in the number of people who inhabit a specific region. This is caused by a higher birth rate and net immigration than the death rate and net emigration. Since the start of the 20th century, the rate of global population growth has increased drastically, growing from just 1.6 billion at the turn of the 20th century to seven billion today.

Sustainable population

A population which has enough natural resources within its environment to thrive, but uses them in a manner which allows for them to be constantly renewed and replaced, thereby ensuring that resources will be available to future generations.

Activities

Brainstorming

◆ In small groups, discuss and make notes on what you know about population. Consider the following:

- What factors contribute to population growth?

- Is population growth a good thing or a bad thing?

- What is happening to the global population?

◆ In pairs create a diamond9 chart to list the factors that contribute to a falling birth-rate.

Research

◆ Create a questionnaire to find out peoples thoughts on population. Are they concerned about population growth?

◆ As a class, find out how many siblings each student has. Are there many that have higher than the 1.8 UK average amount of children?

◆ Choose a European country and research what is happening to its population. Is it growing or declining?

◆ Research what effects a growing population may have on the climate emergency.

Design

◆ Choose one of the articles in this book and create an illustration to highlight the key themes in the article.

◆ Choose one of the articles in this book and create an infographic to show the facts and statistics in the article.

◆ Create a time-line to show the increase in population and illustrate the important dates in history that may have had an effect on the population.

◆ Design a poster on the benefits for having a small family, Consider the effects on the environment as well as the global population.

◆ Design a leaflet or poster on changes that need to be made for the rise in age of the population. What would need to happen to ensure that older people live comfortably?

Oral

◆ In pairs, discuss why you think the birth rate is declining.

◆ As a class, debate the statement 'smaller families mean better lives for all'. Half of the class should argue in favour of the statement and the other against.

◆ In small groups, discuss the issue of depopulation. Does this need to change? Is there an ideal level for population?

◆ In small groups, discuss why you think that the mortality rate has stalled. How does the UK compare to other countries?

◆ In pairs, discuss why you think we have an ageing population. Are there any changes in society that will have to be made to help an older population?

Reading/Writing

◆ Choose one of the articles in this book and write a one-paragraph summary. Pick five key points and list them.

◆ Write a short definition of:

- Population

- Overpopulation

- Depopulation

◆ Write an article for your school newspaper on the decline in birth rate in the UK.

◆ Read 'Whatever happened to 2 point 4 children?' on page 8. Write a short essay on why women are having fewer children.

◆ Write a blog on the life expectancy of people in Japan compared to those in the UK.

◆ Write a short story on what may happen if the population continues to grow. Will it be a wonderful or terrifying tale?

◆ Read *The Children of Men* by PD James. Write a short book review.

Acknowledgements

The publisher is grateful for permission to reproduce the material in this book. While every care has been taken to trace and acknowledge copyright, the publisher tenders its apology for any accidental infringement or where copyright has proved untraceable. The publisher would be pleased to come to a suitable arrangement in any such case with the rightful owner.

Images

Cover image courtesy of iStock. All other images courtesy of Pixabay and Unsplash, except page 37, 38: Freepik

Icons

Icons on pages 24 were made by Freepik from www.freepik.com.

Illustrations

Don Hatcher: pages 23 & 34. Simon Kneebone: pages 8 & 33. Angelo Madrid: pages 5 & 29.

Additional acknowledgements

With thanks to the Independence team: Shelley Baldry, Danielle Lobban, Jackie Staines and Jan Sunderland.

Tracy Biram

Cambridge, January 2020